30119 027 510 99 1

D0715925

York

Da

Local, characterful guides to Britain's special places

Mike Bagshaw

Contributing author
Caroline Mills

EDITION 1

Bradt Travel Guides Ltd, UK
The Globe Pequot Press Inc, USA

Bradt

Yorkshire Dales

Get yourself out of the car, off the tarmac and under the skin of this wonderful place. You will feel cares and troubles drain away as you stride the fells, ride a steam train or snooze under canvas.

1 Burnsall village, Wharfedale. (PTI/A) 2 Full steam ahead over Ribblehead. (AF/A) 3 Luxury yurts are available at Bivouac campsite near Masham. (Y) 4 Extreme cycling on the Three Peaks. (WTY) 5 Hiking along a quiet footpath, Malhamdale. (PH/AWL)

EXPLORING WILD PLACES

The wild is never far away in a place dominated by limestone. It's there to climb up, delve into, walk over or simply sit on to marvel at the landscapes and wildlife of the Yorkshire Dales National Park.

5 Kayaking on the Scar House Reservoir, Nidderdale. (PH/AWL) 6 Otter – a shy river hunter. (S/OT) 7 Two male grouse competing at a lek – a courtship display performed by only three bird species in Britain. (S/E) 8 The world's fastest bird, the peregrine falcon can be spotted anywhere in the Dales. (S/SR) 9 Red grouse is the more famous of the two resident grouse species. (SS)

10 A typical Dales view: Buckden Pike and Upper Wharfedale. (YDNPA) **11** Wain Worth Force, one of the River Swale's many waterfalls near Keld. (VB/BOV) **12** The strenuous sport of fell-running, Malhamdale. (PH/AWL) **13** Pen-y-ghent, the peakiest of the Three Peaks. (YN) **14** Downhill at last: Arten Gill, Dentdale. (VB/BOV)

How did it all happen? George (my then husband) and I wrote the first Bradt guide – about hiking in Peru and Bolivia – on an Amazon river barge, and typed it up on a borrowed typewriter. We had no money for the next two books so George went to work for a printer and was paid in books rather than money.

Forty years on, Bradt publishes over 200 titles that sell all over the world. I still suffer from Imposter Syndrome – how did it all happen? I hadn't even worked in an office before! Well, I've been extraordinarily lucky with the people around me. George provided the belief to get us started (and the mother to run our US office). Then, in 1977, I recruited a helper, Janet Mears, who is still working for us. She and the many dedicated staff who followed have been the foundations on which the company is built. But the bricks and mortar have been our authors and readers. Without them there would be no Bradt Travel Guides. Thank you all for making it happen.

Hilary Bradt

Celebrate our anniversary and get a 40% discount on all titles with the code BRADT40.

Available from www.bradtguides.com

AUTHOR

Mike Bagshaw is a Lancastrian by birth and a zoologist by training. After four years as a student in Sheffield he qualified as a biology teacher and has taught full-time ever since. Initially this took place indoors in school classrooms, but since 1987 he has worked in outdoor education centres, introducing children and adults to the delights of water sports, mountaineering, forest education and how to understand and appreciate the natural world.

In his spare time he has travelled the wild places of the world as a naturalist and explorer, often in a canoe or kayak, and written about his experiences for outdoor magazines. He contributes monthly nature columns to local newspapers and has had a book of poetry published.

CONTRIBUTING AUTHOR

Caroline Mills, author of the Nidderdale chapter, is a freelance writer of travel guides, including the Bradt guide *Slow Cotswolds*, and contributes to various national magazines on travel, food and gardens. Though not officially of Yorkshire stock, she has many family connections with the county she classes as her second 'home'. Having lived in York, she returns to North Yorkshire regularly. Caroline writes, 'It has been great to return "home" for this guide. When you live in an area, it's easy to take your surroundings for granted and stop exploring. Returning to Yorkshire, I've visited with a fresh pair of eyes and have been able to talk with residents about places they didn't know were on their doorstep.'

First edition published April 2014
Bradt Travel Guides Ltd
IDC House, The Vale, Chalfont St Peter, Bucks SL9 9RZ, England
www.bradtguides.com
Print edition published in the USA by The Globe Pequot Press Inc,
PO Box 480, Guilford, Connecticut 06437-0480

Text copyright © 2014 Bradt Travel Guides Ltd
Maps copyright © 2014 Bradt Travel Guides Ltd
Photographs copyright © 2014 Individual photographers (see page 178)
Series Editor: Tim Locke
Project Managers: Maisie Fitzpatrick, Anna Moores and Laura Pidgley
Series Design: Pepi Bluck, Perfect Picture
Cover: Pepi Bluck, Perfect Picture

ISBN: 978 1 84162 549 2 (print)
e-ISBN: 978 1 84162 850 9 (e-pub)
e-ISBN: 978 1 84162 639 0 (mobi)

British Library Cataloguing in Publication Data
A catalogue record for this book is available from the British Library

Front cover image Swaledale, Yorkshire Dales National Park (MKP/A)
Back cover image Footpath sign in Three Peaks Country (YN)
Title page image Cobbled street, Dent (DD)

Photographers
See page 178 for details.

Maps Pepi Bluck, Perfect Picture & David McCutcheon FBCart. S

Typeset from the author's disc by Pepi Bluck, Perfect Picture
Production managed by Jellyfish Print Solutions; printed in the UK
Digital conversion by the Firsty Group

FOREWORD

Gary Verity, Chief Executive of Welcome to Yorkshire

Slow travel is a philosophy that is so natural to Yorkshire that we should have, if it were allowed, copyrighted it. North Yorkshire especially doesn't lend itself to rushing. Why rush when there is so much to take in, to absorb, slowly, and to appreciate? As a sheep farmer in Leyburn in my spare time, I know what a wonderful place it is to be, in liquid sunshine or on a bright and brilliant summer's day. You feel like if you blink you'll miss something, so perish the thought of rushing through. This is why we were so delighted to be involved in the *Slow North Yorkshire* guidebook. Yorkshire is attracting more visitors than ever and we want them to spend more time exploring our wonderful county and to keep coming back (with their friends and family!) to discover new – or rediscover old – favourites. Yorkshire has inspired award-winning writers, artists, photographers and film makers from across the world and the landscape covered in this guide has been widely captured on canvas, celluloid and in thousands of pages of print. Yet nothing can ever re-create the sense of actually being there. For me, the view from Sutton Bank is one of the finest in England – I never tire of seeing it – and you need to have visited it yourself to realise that photos can only do it so much justice. I hope that this guide will take you to many places you have seen on screen or heard about but not actually visited before, and that the experience of seeing them will be something that will stay with you and keep you coming back for years to come. Anyway, enough of my words. You will only fully appreciate how special the people, the landscape and the places of North Yorkshire are by immersing yourself in all they have to offer and by adopting the slower pace of life for which this guide is suited. Savour everything you see, don't rush, for I am sure I will be welcoming you back to Yorkshire soon enough.

ACKNOWLEDGEMENTS

A big thank you goes to all those people that have helped me with this book. All those Yorkshire contributors who shared a little of their lives and passions and allowed me to quote them; Caroline Mills for contributing a chapter of writing; and everyone in the Bradt team, especially Tim Locke, for being so professional and patient.

On the face of it, a Lancastrian 'townie' writing about rural Yorkshire is an unusual phenomenon, but the truth is that I have spent more of my life in this adopted county than in the one of my birth.

My first experience of Yorkshire, a seaside holiday in the late 1960s, was a shocking one; for a ten-year-old boy used to the Gulf Stream waters of north Wales, swimming in the North Sea came as a very rude awakening.

Fast forward a few years and I am back in Dentdale, where we teenagers enjoyed residential stays in the school's country cottage. With hindsight, those first exposures to real country life – windswept hills, clean rivers and undisturbed wildlife were life-changing experiences, for which I am eternally grateful.

That initial love affair with the Yorkshire Dales has been consummated every Easter since, for 30 years, accompanied by a handful of like-minded school friends, and during that time we reckon to have visited just about every hill-top and decent pub available. That, coupled with my 21 years living and working in the North York Moors, led me to believe that I knew pretty much all there was to know about North Yorkshire. How wrong I was.

The welcome opportunity to write this guide has allowed me to see familiar places in a new light, and discover corners I had unwittingly missed. It also gave me the incentive to go and do some of those things that I'd always promised myself, like watch an early-morning black grouse lek, or brave the descent of Gaping Gill cavern. Best of all, it's re-kindled my desire to go out exploring, and see what else I might have missed in this wonderful county.

DEDICATION

To my wife Lois who has been unofficial researcher, typist, editor, proofreader and general life coach for the past year; without her this book would not have been possible.

Mike Bagshaw

CONTENTS

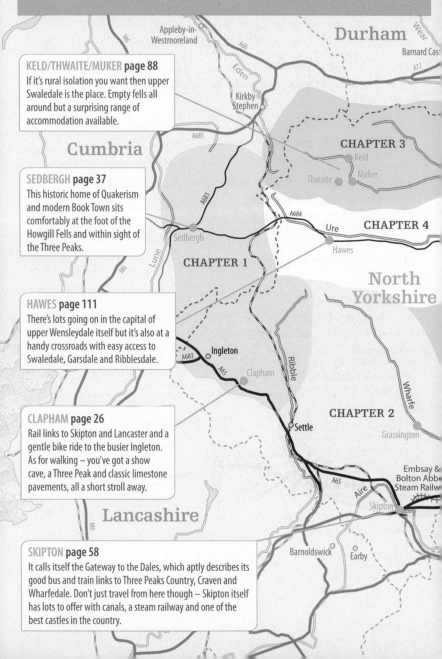

Suggested places to base yourself

These bases make ideal starting points for exploring localities the Slow way.

KELD/THWAITE/MUKER page 88
If it's rural isolation you want then upper Swaledale is the place. Empty fells all around but a surprising range of accommodation available.

SEDBERGH page 37
This historic home of Quakerism and modern Book Town sits comfortably at the foot of the Howgill Fells and within sight of the Three Peaks.

HAWES page 111
There's lots going on in the capital of upper Wensleydale itself but it's also at a handy crossroads with easy access to Swaledale, Garsdale and Ribblesdale.

CLAPHAM page 26
Rail links to Skipton and Lancaster and a gentle bike ride to the busier Ingleton. As for walking – you've got a show cave, a Three Peak and classic limestone pavements, all a short stroll away.

SKIPTON page 58
It calls itself the Gateway to the Dales, which aptly describes its good bus and train links to Three Peaks Country, Craven and Wharfedale. Don't just travel from here though – Skipton itself has lots to offer with canals, a steam railway and one of the best castles in the country.

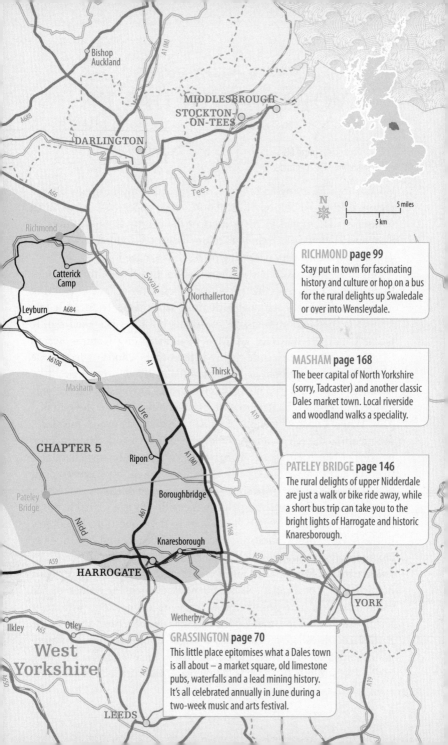

RICHMOND page 99

Stay put in town for fascinating history and culture or hop on a bus for the rural delights up Swaledale or over into Wensleydale.

MASHAM page 168

The beer capital of North Yorkshire (sorry, Tadcaster) and another classic Dales market town. Local riverside and woodland walks a speciality.

PATELEY BRIDGE page 146

The rural delights of upper Nidderdale are just a walk or bike ride away, while a short bus trip can take you to the bright lights of Harrogate and historic Knaresborough.

GRASSINGTON page 70

This little place epitomises what a Dales town is all about – a market square, old limestone pubs, waterfalls and a lead mining history. It's all celebrated annually in June during a two-week music and arts festival.

CHAPTER 5

N

0   5 miles
0   5 km

YORKSHIRE DALES

North Yorkshire is England's largest county, and an astonishingly diverse region. In the first edition of this book, which appeared as *Slow North Yorkshire*, I attempted to cover most of the county in one volume. A Slow appraisal of a place shouldn't skim, but needs to look at the detail, so inevitably some very deserving places didn't make it in.

This new book covers the western section, that area of the Pennines traditionally known as the Yorkshire Dales, with all but one sitting predominantly in the national park of the same name. Nidderdale was left out in the cold on the park's inception, but has since been rightly granted its own status as an Area of Outstanding Natural Beauty (AONB). I have been a little flighty with borders, choosing to include the whole of the national park, and consequently allowing a chunk of Cumbria to stow away on board; likewise, some of Wensleydale features in the Nidderdale chapter because of its failure to make the national park. Where I do have feelings of guilt and regret are towards the places not mentioned, such as old West Riding, new South Yorkshire and even pockets of North Yorkshire; there will be corners and many characters that I've had to leave out. The eastern side of the county has been dealt with separately in *Slow North York Moors & Yorkshire Wolds*.

What makes the Yorkshire Dales so special? Why is it visited so much and written about so often? The answers to these questions lie not just in the obvious observations of space, natural beauty and breathtaking landscape; it involves the culture of the place as well – the people. Dales folk are often old-fashioned but proud of it, they see it as an attribute, not a fault. While many places are rediscovering the values of the traditional, real and genuine, and renewing connections with their history and landscape, many parts of the Dales never lost them in the first place. So-called progress has brought us cheap, mass-produced goods sold in supermarkets the size of villages and even bigger shopping malls. Thankfully, a backlash is taking place, and rural North Yorkshire is at the forefront of the push to preserve those things that make places different, interesting and … well, real. Folk are fighting hard to keep their village shops open, promote locally produced, high-quality food and drink, and encourage their own artists and artisans. These are the special people – the brewers, potters, shop-keepers, cheese-makers, farmers, wood-carvers, butchers, bakers and candlestick makers – that have managed to capture a little of the essence of their corner of this singular county, and enable you to feel it, smell it, taste it or even take a little of it away with you.

I hope this book inspires you, not just to read about the Yorkshire Dales, but to live it – to come and meet these people, spend some Slow time where they live and get to know it as they do.

THE SLOW MINDSET

Hilary Bradt, Founder, Bradt Travel Guides

We shall not cease from exploration
And the end of all our exploring
Will be to arrive where we started
And know the place for the first time.

T S Eliot 'Little Gidding', *Four Quartets*

This series evolved, slowly, from a Bradt editorial meeting when we started to explore ideas for guides to our favourite country – Great Britain. We wanted to get away from the usual 'top sights' formula and encourage our authors to bring out the nuances and local differences that make up a sense of place – such things as food, history, nature, geology, or local people and what makes them tick. So without our realising it at the time, we had defined 'Slow Travel', or at least our concept of it. For the beauty of the Slow movement is that there is no fixed definition; we adapt the philosophy to fit our individual needs and aspirations. Thus Carl Honoré, author of *In Praise of Slow*, writes: 'The Slow Movement is a cultural revolution against the notion that faster is always better. It's not about doing everything at a snail's pace, it's about seeking to do everything at the right speed. Savouring the hours and minutes rather than just counting them. Doing everything as well as possible, instead of as fast as possible. It's about quality over quantity in everything from work to food to parenting.' And travel.

So take time to explore. Don't rush it, get to know an area – and the people who live there – and you'll be as delighted as the authors by what you find.

Climb a few hills, stroll through the woods and meditate in a ruined abbey, eat a pork pie by the river from the village butchers and finish the day in an old stone pub, with a glass of your favourite tipple and a crackling fire to toast your feet on – I can think of worse ways of passing time.

A DALES TIMELINE

For the Yorkshire Dales there have been four milestone events. The first of these moments was a long one, the Carboniferous period lasting 140 million years in fact. During this time, the overwhelmingly dominant rock of the Dales, its limestone, was laid down, as multi-layered coral reef in a shallow tropical sea.

Ten thousand years ago, the next big event was drawing to a close, as the Devensian ice finally retreated, to reveal the shapes it had carved into the underlying land surface; classic 'U'-shaped valleys, ice-plucked crags with cascading waterfalls and bare, soil-less hill-tops.

Man's first real impact came in the Bronze Age, when a vast, blanketing wildwood was cleared for agriculture, and finally, all the newly revealed features were named by the Vikings just over a thousand years ago. Fell, dale, foss, ghyll and beck are all pure lingua-Scandinavia, as are most of Yorkshire's town and village names.

Obviously, a lot has happened since the Danes arrived – castle-building in Norman times, lead mining, and the Industrial Revolution for instance – but 1954 will always be a particularly important year with the formation of the Yorkshire Dales National Park. As in all 13 other national parks, the authority is charged with maintaining and enhancing the landscape, nature, culture and history of the park, for us visitors, and the people that live in it, to enjoy. In striving towards these ideals, it has made itself a champion of all things traditional and sustainable, and a tremendous source of information and expertise for those of us that wish to go Slow in the Dales.

"The national park is the champion of all things traditional and sustainable."

What they do particularly well is enable travel and discovery without a car. **Cycling** is strongly encouraged, both on roads (www.cyclethedales.org.uk) and off-road on mountain bikes (www.yorkshiredales.org.uk). For many other outdoor activities, the website, or friendly staff in the visitor centres, will direct you to clubs and national governing bodies, but for one fairly new and enjoyable outdoor pastime, they are being a lot more pro-active. **Geocaching** is a sort of computerised treasure hunting, using GPS (global positioning system) receivers, and is a great activity for families, especially those with children who need to be given a reason for setting out on a good walk. You can download information on to your own GPS in one of the visitor centres, or hire one for a very reasonable charge.

One final activity that the national park does not mention at all, possibly because these days it seems a little radical and alternative, is **wild swimming**. All the main rivers in the Dales have hidden corners where the water is clean, clear, the right depth and safe enough to swim in, and one or two, the Wharfe and Swale in particular, boast some of the best wild bathing in the country. If you want advice on where to swim, then see ⚐ www.wildswimming.co.uk or ⚐ www.river-swimming.co.uk, but I prefer a more impromptu approach. If I happen to be walking along a riverbank on a warm, sunny day and find a likely and private place, I'll slip off my clothes and plunge in. If you've not done it, have a try – it's one of the most refreshing and life-affirming experiences you can have.

For **information** about the Yorkshire Dales National Park before you visit, go online to their website, ⚐ www.yorkshiredales.org.uk, or get hold of a copy of their annual guide/newspaper, *The Visitor*.

FLOWERS OF THE DALES

Lime-rich soil, a history of traditional non-intensive agriculture and lots of rain: these are the three blessings bestowed on the Yorkshire Dales that allow a fabulously rich flora to bloom in the spring and summer months.

Down in the valleys, away from the biting wind and chance of a late blizzard, early March can see odd pioneers like butterbur and coltsfoot appearing on roadside verges, but late March is when the real display starts. A bright, crisp, early-spring-day stroll along an old sunken lane like Thoresby Lane near Castle Bolton (see page 123) or Howgill Lane near Appletreewick (see page 74) can be an ideal way to celebrate the end of winter. Yellow celandines and white wood anemones pepper the track bank like scattered stars, still-furled cuckoo-pint flowers arrow their way upwards and the humble mochatel, a particular favourite of mine, hides behind more extrovert blooms. I love alternative country names for flowers and the mochatel's pseudonym of 'town hall clock' is an elegantly descriptive one. The flower stalk stands vertical and produces at its tip four outward-facing green circular flowers all at 90 degrees to their neighbour, and a fifth as an afterthought pointing straight upwards. All they need are tiny numerals and hands and the model would be perfect.

May is the time for the woodlands of the region, when the great floral carpets are unrolled; wild garlic or ramsons and the incomparable bluebell. There cannot be many better displays anywhere in the country than Skipton Woods (see page 59) or Hag Wood near Richmond (see page 100). Out in the fields, hawthorn hedges paint lines of white may blossom up hillsides and wet roadsides dance with bobbing heads of water avens.

If you can only visit the Dales once in the year to experience its flowers, then June has to be the time. This is when the display is at its peak: daylight hours are at their maximum and plant growth is so fast you can almost hear it. This is when the iconic limestone flowers appear, trademark verge and hedge blues like meadow cranesbill and nettle-leaved bellflower, traditional hayfield species including yellow rattle and betony, and the real stars of the show, the orchids. Many of the family are lime loving (calcicoles) so it is no surprise that more than ten species of orchid grow within the national park. All are beautiful, none is very common and some are extremely rare.

The lady's slipper orchid is arguably the best looking and without doubt the rarest flower of all: only one native wild lady's slipper orchid plant exists in Britain and it grows in a secret ash-wood location somewhere in the Craven and Wharfedale locale. In pre-Victorian times this orchid was also found in Derbyshire, Durham and Cumbria but was never common. Wholesale picking for markets and uprooting for collections was its downfall, the attraction, of course, being its stunning appearance. The maroon perianth crowns the golden-yellow shoe-shaped lip which gives the plant all of its names; *Cyripedium calceolus* literally means 'little shoe of Venus', and 'Mary's shoe' is a vernacular Yorkshire name.

Now other lady's slippers grow in one or two dales and Cumbrian woods but these are all artificially propagated from seeds collected since 1987 from the one 'wild' plant. Natural England is co-ordinating this Species Recovery Programme, which is now starting to blossom – literally. It takes 11 years for a lady's slipper plant to flower once established, and in 2000 the first of the new scheme's offspring did just that near Ingleton.

Let us hope that the efforts of the scientists are successful – that these magnificent flowers return to their old haunts, no longer secret and guarded, and we can all marvel at the plant that so nearly disappeared.

Every summer the national park organises a **Flowers of the Dales Festival** with nearly a hundred events: walks, meetings, talks and such like, across the whole park. The festival runs from the beginning of May until the end of September and is an excellent way to learn about and celebrate the flora of the Dales. For details contact the Yorkshire Dales Millennium Trust (01524 251002 www.ydmt.org).

SHEEP OF THE DALES

'Look Mum, a Rastafarian goat!' The **Wensleydale** sheep, so insulted by the teenager leaning over a wall near Hawes, tried not to look offended, but in truth it was one of the oddest looking farm animals that I've ever seen. Wensleydales are the tallest British breed of sheep, but they still manage to grow a full-body set of dreadlocks, so long that they trail on the ground, and make the most valuable sheep's wool in the world. Sometimes called 'poor man's mohair,' it is prized by local knitters; the breed almost became extinct in the 1970s, but was saved by the Rare Breeds Survival Trust.

For sheer numbers though, no breed of sheep can match the **Swaledale**, not just in Yorkshire but in all of upland northern England. The high fells and moors are dominated by these hardy black-faced and horned ewes to such an extent that a Swaledale sheep's head was chosen as the emblem of the Yorkshire Dales National Park. These days they are crossed with Texel rams to produce good meat lambs, but back in the 1940s they were usually pure-bred.

Transport was more traditional then as well, as Stanley Thackray, the last living drover in Wharfedale, remembers: 'We would walk the sheep and cattle down the dale roads to market in Skipton, yes – our animals and some neighbours', for fourpence an animal. My father had a very good dog in the 40s so we were often called on, especially after another drover, Old Jossy, died. Joe Ibbotson had a cattle wagon, but there was no petrol, it being the war years, so walking the beasts was the only way. It all stopped about 1950 when folk got hold of petrol again, and the roads became too busy – yes.'

Times have changed. These days the price of lamb is so low that most hill farmers can only survive with the help of large government subsidies and each sheep costs the tax-payer more to produce than its meat and wool are actually worth. This ridiculous and unsustainable situation has prompted some commentators to suggest a drastic scaling down of hill-sheep farming. The removal of hundreds of thousands of sets of nibbling teeth would save millions of pounds and also allow the natural vegetation of the Yorkshire Dales to return. Perhaps in a hundred years time the Three Peaks will float majestically above a sea of forest and the emblem of the national park will be an oak tree.

THERE'S LEAD IN THEM THERE HILLS

Yorkshire lead can be found in the paint on the frescoes of Pompeii, in the plumbing of classical Rome and on the medieval roofs of Antwerp and Bordeaux. The fascinating story of how it found its way to all of these places starts millions of years ago. Geological movements caused thousands of small cracks to form in the limestone surface of the north Pennines, which filled with mineral-rich hot water from deep below the earth's crust. When it cooled it deposited crystals of various minerals, including galena or lead sulphide, and this is the ore that has been extracted on a small scale for thousands of years. We know that the Romans delved here because a block or 'pig' of lead was found stamped with the Emperor Trajan's name. Later, the rich monasteries at Fountains, Rievaulx and Jervaulx kept records of their 15th-century trade with Belgium and France.

Lead mining went large-scale between 1650 and 1900, and its impact on the landscape and rural society was devastating. Valleys that had previously only known woodland crafts and sheep farming now became brutal and polluted industrial centres. Forests were felled and hillsides shaved of peat to fuel the furnaces, and miles of tunnel were blasted out underground. One particularly destructive practice was called 'hushing', where a beck was dammed to form a reservoir above a hillside with a known lead vein. The dam was deliberately breached to cause a flash flood which would scour off all the surface soil and rock thus exposing the valuable seam beneath.

Thousands of outsiders moved into the Dales, living in squalor for the most part, sometimes ten or 12 to a two-roomed cottage with shared beds slept in on a rota. A whole sub-culture developed, almost with its own language. A young miner would for instance, strike a 'bar-gain', or join a *"Every cloud does have a silver lining, in this case it is the spring sandwort."* 'gang' who would work underground on a 'stope'. 'Bouse' would be taken out by 'kibble' or 'whim' to fill a 'bouseteam'. This was emptied on to the 'dressing floor', the 'deads' were rejected and the remainder was 'spalled' and 'bukkered' to make it small enough to be sieved in a 'hotching tub' and then the 'slime' collected in a 'running buddle'. The ore was then 'smelted' and cast into a 'pig'. Got that? Good. Working life started at ten years old and ended on average (life that is) at 45. Life expectancy was so short because of long working hours, bad air in the mines, poisonous fumes from the smelters, tuberculosis from cramped living, and general poverty. Some miners were so poor they knitted clothes as they walked to work to sell for a few extra pennies.

Faced with this human cost, I can't help feeling that the collapse of lead mining in the early 20th century was a blessing. Virtually no veterans with a first-hand memory of the industry survive, and the economy of the Dales has returned to sheep and, latterly, tourism. Socially, outside of museums and archives, it's as if nothing had ever happened, but up on the fell-sides, scars will take longer to heal. The problem is that the lead that still remains in the 'hushed' areas and vast spoil heaps, being poisonous, stopped the vegetation regenerating. The moors around Greenhow in Nidderdale and above Grassington in Wharfedale are grim, bare and uninviting places, but nothing compared with the north side of Swaledale. The walking-guide guru, Alfred Wainwright, deliberately routed his Coast to Coast Walk through the worst of the damaged landscape because he felt people needed to see the consequences of irresponsible land use.

Every cloud does have a silver lining though, and in this case it is *Minuartia verna*, the spring sandwort, a beautiful and rare plant; rare, that is, virtually everywhere except on lead-mine spoil heaps. This is one of the few British plants tolerant to high levels of lead and its neat cushions are sometimes the only life in a heavy metal desert.

CAR-FREE TRAVEL

Most people get here and travel around within the area by car. However, a growing number of visitors to the Dales are doing it without their cars. Car-free travel is at the root of the Slow mindset. And, planned well and done properly, can be a really liberating experience. The national park authority are very supportive of this idea – not surprisingly, they want more people in the park but fewer cars, so they have a whole section of their website devoted to encouraging this.

TRAINS

As you would expect from a mountainous region, railways tend to skirt the edges, getting you to outlying towns and villages like Skipton, Settle, Clapham, Richmond, Northallerton, Harrogate and Knaresborough, but not into the interior. The one glorious exception is the Settle to Carlisle line (see page 58), which ploughs straight through the middle of the Dales, giving access to Horton in Ribblesdale, Dentdale and Garsdale/Wensleydale heads.

A couple of short, private railways add to the picture, but because they are not fully linked to the National Rail system, they are not of huge use to car-free travellers. To be fair though, the operators of the Embsay line are working hard to join it up to Skipton, as are the Wensleydale Railway Association to Northallerton.

We could moan at length about the inadequacies of our National Rail system (and I often do) but one aspect they need hearty congratulations for is the free transport of bikes rule. This facility opens up so many doors for cyclists, who either don't own a car or are tired of doing circular routes back to the hire shop. Using the train to gain altitude and save your legs is a good ploy; you could for instance, take your bike on the train to Ribblehead and freewheel back to Settle or Clapham via Ingleton. Likewise, Dent Station gives a nice quiet run down to Sedbergh and Oxenhome Station beyond. Garsdale Station allows a similar downhill trip to Kirby Stephen.

BUSES

Without a bike in tow you also have the bus network at your disposal (some buses advertise bike transport but as there is a limit of three per bus you can't rely on it). Peripheral towns usually have very good bus links to the outside, especially if they have no railway station:

- **Ingleton** Five buses a day from Lancaster (80) and six from Settle (581).
- **Leyburn** Ten buses a day from Bedale (156,157) and nine from Richmond (159).
- **Masham** Four buses a day from Bedale (144) and six from Ripon (138, 159).
- **Pateley Bridge** Hourly bus from Harrogate (24).
- **Richmond** Very regular buses from Darlington (X26, X27, 28) and eight buses a day from Northallerton (54, 55).
- **Ripon** Very regular buses from Harrogate (36) and six a day each from Thirsk and Northallerton (70, 170)
- **Sedbergh** Eight buses a day from Kendal (564) and four from Kirby Stephen (564).

All the other smaller places up the Dales are served by the **Dales Explorer Bus** (⌂ www.dalesbus.org). Almost every hamlet gets a visit at some time, even if it is just once a week in summer, like poor old Scar House in Nidderdale. Many routes operate weekdays, and all year round, but quite a few extra leisure services are put on for the summer months (Easter to October). And these are usually only Sundays and bank holidays. All the details, including maps and timetables, are available to download from the website, or as a free booklet from ⌂ www.wymetro.com.

Other entertaining summer additions are the two brilliant **vintage tour buses**. The Wensleydale bus (127) runs on Tuesdays from Ripon, right up the dale to Garsdale Station (after a two hour break in Hawes). Also on Tuesdays, the 569 Cumbria Classic coach runs from Hawes to Kirby Stephen.

Various fare concessions are out there, and probably the best on offer is the **Dales Rover Ticket**, giving you unlimited bus journeys for the day within the Dales, and deals from many local businesses like cafés, pubs, B&Bs and attractions. If they display a 'Dales Bus Discount Scheme' sticker you will get some freebee or other, even if it's only a cup of tea.

BOAT TRIPS

Unless you count the rowing boats on the River Nidd at Knaresborough, the Leeds and Liverpool Canal at Skipton is the one and only boating venue in the Dales, but it does offer a variety of options. You can join half-hour or one-hour trips in and around town, or hire a boat for a day, weekend or entire week. Westwards is the more rural and unspoilt direction to sail from Skipton, but even this choice turns away from the

Dales and into the lowlands, on its journey towards Lancashire; a tour of farm country – nice and certainly Slow, if tame.

- **Pennine Boat Trips** Coach St, Skipton ☎ 01756 790829 🖰 www.canaltrips.co.uk. One-hour public cruises on a 58-foot narrowboat. Catered private charters available. Also has self-drive five-seater motorboats.
- **Pennine Cruisers** Coach St, Skipton ☎ 01756 795478 🖰 www.penninecruisers.com. Half-hour public cruises around the back of the castle. Daily self-drive hire of 30-foot narrowboat for up to ten people, also evenings. Half-week and full-week holidays with four or eight berths.
- **Snaygill Boats** Bradley ☎ 01756 795150 🖰 www.snaygillboats.co.uk. A similar day and holiday hire service to Pennine Cruisers, but from a village two miles away.

HOW THIS BOOK IS ARRANGED

MAPS

The colour map at the front of this book shows the area of land that falls within each chapter. The chapters themselves begin with a more detailed map bearing numbered points which correspond to numbered headings in the text. Featured walks have an even larger scale map accompanying them.

By far the most complete and useful maps for walking, cycling, horse-riding and general sightseeing are the OS 1:25,000 scale Explorer series. Those covering the region described in this book are:

- OL2 Yorkshire Dales – Southern & Western areas.
- OL19 Howgill Fells and Upper Eden Valley.
- OL30 Yorkshire Dales – Northern & Central areas.
- 298 Nidderdale.

Other maps specifically designed for hill-walkers, fell-runners or cyclists, with bags of useful extra information, are produced by Harveys (🖰 www.harveysmaps.co.uk). Their Dales titles include:

- Mountain Map 1:40,000 Yorkshire Dales.
- Superwalker 1:25,000 Howgill Fells.
- Superwalker 1:25,000 Yorkshire Dales Three Peaks.
- Dales Way 1:40,000.
- Nidderdale Way 1:40,000.
- *Eight Walks Centred On* series – day walks around popular dales towns and villages.

Also, look out for the classic series of local walk maps hand-drawn in black and red ink by Arthur Gemmell, and unchanged in style for nearly half a century.

ACCOMMODATION

Accommodation has been recommended on the basis of location and because it embraces a Slow approach either in its 'green' ethos or its overall feel.

Hotels, B&Bs and self-catering options are indicated by the symbol ♠ after town and village headings, and campsites by ⚑, with a cross-reference to the full listing under *Accommodation* pages 172–8.

FOOD & DRINK

Recommended places for food and drink include restaurants, cafés, pubs, farm shops, delis and suchlike. Inclusion is my choice alone with no charge having been paid by the outlet. My selection criteria are quality, value and 'Slow' credentials such as home-grown vegetables or meat from named local farms. Food miles are important but I was willing to make exceptions – the Russian Tea Rooms in Skipton for instance.

"I'm very fussy about my pubs and like them to be as 'unimproved' as possible. Rest assured that every pub or inn included serves cask beer, usually brewed locally."

I'm very fussy about my pubs and like them to be as 'unimproved' as possible, not exclusively foodie and a genuine part of the community that they are in – in short, a proper local. As for beer, I will not allow keg or smooth-flow liquids to pass my lips, so you can rest assured that every pub or inn included serves cask beer, usually brewed locally.

REQUEST FOR FEEDBACK

The Yorkshire Dales are stuffed with people who have specialist knowledge on their part of the county, and although we've done our best to check our facts there are bound to be errors as well as the inevitable omissions of really special places. You can post your thoughts, comments and recommendations, and read the latest feedback from other readers online at ⌂ www.bradtupdates.com/yorkshiredales.

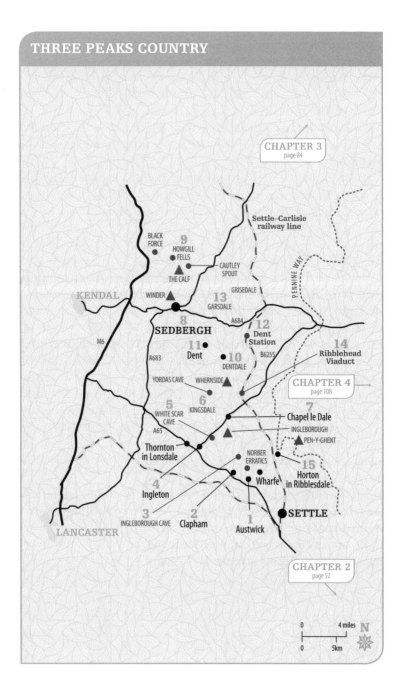

CHAPTER 3
page 84

Settle–Carlisle
railway line

BLACK
FORCE

9
HOWGILL
FELLS

CAUTLEY
SPOUT

THE CALF

PENNINE WAY

KENDAL

WINDER

GRISEDALE

13
GARSDALE

A684

8
SEDBERGH

12
Dent
Station

M6

11
Dent

10
DENTDALE

B6255

14
Ribblehead
Viaduct

A683

YORDAS CAVE

WHERNSIDE

5
WHITE SCAR
CAVE

6
KINGSDALE

CHAPTER 4
page 108

A65

Chapel le Dale

7

INGLEBOROUGH

PEN-Y-GHENT

Thornton
in Lonsdale

NORBER
ERRATICS

15
Horton
in Ribblesdale

4
Ingleton

Wharfe

3
INGLEBOROUGH CAVE

2
Clapham

1
Austwick

SETTLE

LANCASTER

CHAPTER 2
page 52

0   4 miles

0   5km

N

1
THREE PEAKS COUNTRY

Some of the highest land in Yorkshire lies on the western side of the Yorkshire Dales (which actually stray into Cumbria), where the rivers Dee, Skirfare, Greta and Ribble bubble into life. It is an area dominated by three great, brooding hills, **Whernside**, **Ingleborough** and **Pen-y-ghent**, that collectively give this area its unofficial name. Ironically, none of these flat-topped heights could remotely be called a peak but a much-tramped long-distance challenge walk linking the three coined the name and it has stuck.

The legendary walking-book author Alfred Wainwright, in his 1970 guide *Walks in Limestone Country*, said of the area: 'This is a region unique, without a counterpart, but its charms are shyly hidden. Those who seek and find them are often enslaved, yet few visitors come looking.' He would probably be astonished and appalled at the numbers of visitors that do come now, but his observation that a little bit of searching can reveal enchanting hidden places still holds true. Some of my first real exploring as a schoolboy was done here, and the hidden places that I discovered then have left indelible marks, and remain very special to me.

"Some of my first real exploring as a schoolboy was done here, and the hidden places that I discovered then have left indelible marks, and remain very special to me."

This is not as uniform a region as the eastern Dales, but an area of borders, watersheds and transformations. Even before the 1974 county boundary changes bit off a huge chunk of the North Riding and called it Cumbria, Lancashire was never far away, and the local Yorkshire accent has a distinct 'lanky' twang to it. Most of the rivers flow west, to join the Lune, and eventually Morecambe Bay; and where the limestone runs out, the hills develop a distinctly Lake District feel to them.

SELF-POWERED TRAVEL

CYCLING

Two long-distance road routes find themselves skirting the Three Peaks. The **Yorkshire Dales Cycleway** and **Pennine Cycleway** join forces to creep up Kingsdale and plummet down Deepdale. When they reach the bottom of Dentdale they part company, the former heading down the dale to Sedbergh and the latter uphill to Hawes.

It is no surprise that official routes are well represented in **Dentdale**, because its network of relatively flat and quiet lanes just beg to be biked around. The national park's **Cycle the Dales** people have recognised this with a 'family ride' circuit of 13 or 19 miles up one side of this picturesque dale and back down the other. You can start anywhere *en route* but Dent village or Sedbergh would make sense, or of course Dent Station if you arrived by train. If you want more of a workout, then their 25-mile route linking Sedbergh, Kirkby Lonsdale and Dentdale takes in an uphill leg traversing the hidden Valley of Barbondale – hard work, but worth it for the dramatic scenery.

Off-road options are not as extensive here as in other parts of the Dales: no big forests or networks of old mine tracks and sadly, many of the green lanes that should be ideal for biking have been irreparably damaged by 4x4 vehicles and trail bikes. However some rewarding rides of varying difficulty are described in a whole library of guidebooks as well as on the **MTB the Dales** section of the national park website. The latter features a good, testing 19-mile circumnavigation of Pen-y-ghent and a severe expedition over the Howgills, but the one they call Tunnels and Bridges suits me best. It is a fairly forgiving 12-mile tour of the bridleways around Clapham and Austwick. For those with a competitive edge, and a touch of lunacy, the 38-mile **Three Peaks Cyclocross** race takes place every September.

Finally, the **upper reaches of Garsdale and Dentdale** have some quiet and really enjoyable rides that are a mixture of track and tarmac, with

---

i **TOURIST INFORMATION**

Horton Pen-y-ghent Café ✆ 01729 860333
Ingleton Main car park ✆ 015242 41049
Sedbergh Dales and Lakes Book Centre, 72 Main St ✆ 015396 20125

the advantage that they are accessible by rail. You could arrive by train at either Garsdale or Dent station and finish your ride at the other, saving a slog over the Coal Road at the end of the day.

HORSERIDING

There are no trekking or riding stables in the region but riders with their own horses can follow the route of the newly opened Pennine Bridleway which skirts the top of Dentdale and Garsdale *en route* to Kirkby Stephen.

WALKING

The scope for exploring on foot here is extensive, from the three official long-distance paths that pass through the region, the **Ribble Way**, **Pennine Way** and **Dales Way**, to the scores of shorter rambles and ambles you'll find described in leaflets which you can pick up at national park and tourist information centres.

The best known is the **Three Peaks walk** itself; an unofficial 24-mile challenge of Whernside, Ingleborough and Pen-y-ghent. Horton in Ribblesdale is the traditional start point, especially if you wish to be registered in the 'club' by finishing within the allotted 12 hours, but you could start and finish anywhere along the route. If, like me, your preferred walks avoid other people then this is not the route for you as the Three Peaks, both individually and collectively, are extremely popular. The footpaths along the route hold the dubious distinction of suffering the worst erosion of any in the country.

"Ingleborough is a hill that's packed with interest from top to bottom: limestone pavements, disappearing rivers and an Iron Age fort."

One solution to the crowd problem could be to reach the summits individually and by different routes to the 'challenge', because these are three magnificent eminences that each deserve a visit. **Whernside**, to my mind, is best tackled from Whernside Manor in Dentdale, up the bridleway to 'Boot of the Wold' then over open fell-side to the summit via the tarns. This is the highest and quietest of the peaks – relish the solitude. A direct descent west takes you into Deepdale where you can hitch down the road or follow beck-side footpaths to your start. **Pen-y-ghent** is the peakiest of the three, neat and well defined. My choice would always be to ascend its precipitous southern nose, from Horton if I've arrived by train, but preferably from Silverdale Road if I have my own transport. This latter option allows a horseshoe walk taking in Plover Hill and returning to the road via Lockley Beck. **Ingleborough** is a hill that's packed with interest from top to bottom. Limestone pavements, disappearing rivers, potholes, an Iron Age fort on the top – and you don't even have to make a round walk of it. Just start at Ingleton, walk the direct path to the summit, then down via Gaping Gill and Ingleborough Cave to descend into the oasis of Clapham village, where a surprisingly regular bus service gets you back to Ingleton.

For those that like someone else to do their navigating for them, **guided walks** are available free from the Friends of the Settle–Carlisle line (✆ 01729 825454 ⌂ www.settle-carlisle.org) and Dalesbus (see page 17) or, for a fee, from the National Park Ranger Service (✆ 0300 456 0030 ⌂ www.yorkshiredales.org.uk). The national park also suggests some **linear walks** incorporating a bus or train to return you to your start point. There is only one wheelchair-accessible route, a 600-yard length of path at Killington New Bridge Nature Reserve near Sedbergh.

Finally, three of my favourites: **Flinter Gill** and **Dentdale** (a five-mile, not too strenuous circuit – see page 43); **Carlingill** and **Blackforce** (a deceptively testing scramble in the Howgills – see page 40); and **Crummack Dale** (a gentle historical potter from Austwick – see page 25).

THE SOUTHERN FRINGE

Ingleborough's flanks mark the southwestern boundary of the Yorkshire Dales National Park and it is here that the villages of **Austwick** and **Clapham** nestle beneath limestone crags by the centuries-old coach route from Skipton to Kendal, now the A65.

A few miles further west, this road crosses the River Greta where the small town of **Ingleton** clings to the valley side. Once a busy quarrying and mining community, Ingleton is now the caving capital of Britain and largest 'town' in the locality.

1 AUSTWICK & AROUND

🏠 **Traddock Hotel** (see page 172)

Like many place names in North Yorkshire, this one is Viking in origin, but unusually it was not given by the Danes colonising from the east.

The Lancashire coast Vikings were Norwegian, and the furthest they settled up this valley was here, hence Austwick, or 'East Farmstead'. With their pervading sense of solid antiquity, the buildings in and around the village green look as if they've been standing in the Pennine drizzle for centuries. Many structures date from the 1600s, including the fine restored medieval cross on the green.

For me though, Austwick's best feature is the glorious walking country just to the north, in the tiny valley of Crummack Dale and the gentle hills that encircle it. **Norber** barely qualifies as a hill in its own right; it is really just an extended spur from the Ingleborough massif, but geologists get particularly excited about it because of a group of scattered boulders on its eastern slope. The **Norber Erratics**, as they are known because they don't really belong here, are blocks of a hard, dark rock called greywacke, some the size of small buildings, that were carried up the hill by a wayward glacier 10,000 years ago, and marooned when the ice melted.

"This is excellent, short-distance rambling territory with an intricate network of paths and bridleways, a relic from the pre-Tudor monastic sheep estates."

The summit plateau of Norber is dotted with cairns, probably placed here by shepherds in years past as landmarks. They did not, however, do their job for one 18th-century farmer, Robin Proctor, whose horse was trained to take him home after a skinful in the Gamecock. At the end of a particularly heavy night he mounted the wrong horse which didn't know the route and promptly walked him off the top of the crag, which bears his name in memorial. **Robin Proctor's Scar** marks the precipitous southern end of the Norber.

If Farmer Proctor's fate does not entice you up to the tops, then the valley bottom is the place for you. This is excellent, short-distance rambling territory with an intricate network of paths and bridleways, a relic from the pre-Tudor monastic sheep estates. Sunken walled lanes weave their way between tiny meadows, and cross Austwick Beck repeatedly on ancient single-stoned 'clapper' bridges. The beck itself is remarkable, as it emerges fully formed from a cave at the dale head, provides a couple of inviting swimming holes and a waterfall or two lower down, before dwindling to a trickle just before the serene and snoozy hamlet of Wharfe.

Before you make your way back to Austwick, it is well worth detouring south to Oxenber and Wharfe woods. These are a double rarity, woodlands on limestone pavement, and very old, a combination that makes them floristically very rich. A large proportion of the woodland is hazel coppice, and local people still have ancient commoners' rights of not just sheep grazing, but also nut gathering. Although privately owned, these woods are open access land and walkers are allowed anywhere within them.

¶ FOOD & DRINK

Feizor Refreshments Home Barn, Feizor LA2 8DF ☎ 01729 824114. A legendary little farm tea room. Cyclists divert here to call for a cuppa and locals walk over from Austwick for snacks.
The Traddock Graystonber Lane, Austwick LA2 8BY ☎ 01524 251224 ⌂ www. thetraddock.co.uk. A hotel serving really high-quality lunches and evening meals. They also do teas, coffees and snacks at other times of day.

2 CLAPHAM

Walk a longish mile west of Austwick, and you will find yourself among the buildings of its more popular sister, Clapham, stretched out along the sides of a chuckling beck. Although about the same size as Austwick it has far more facilities for visitors; its shops, cafés, car park, pub and information point all contribute to making Clapham a very busy little village at times.

This tourist drawing-power was boosted significantly by the opening of the Victorian railway station, the trains delivering carriage loads of visitors to the newly discovered **Ingleborough Cave** a mile up the valley of Clapham Beck. The cave lies on the land belonging to the Ingleborough Estate which, in the 18th century, belonged to the Farrer family. They had constructed what is still by far the biggest building in the village, **Ingleborough Hall** (now an outdoor education centre; see page 28), but it was a great-grandson, Reginald Farrer, who had the most lasting influence. He was a botanist and plant collector in the early years of the 20th century, who brought back many exotic species from the Himalayas and planted them in the estate grounds. He could be very imaginative in his planting techniques, and once fired alpine rock plant seeds at a cliff face from a shotgun to give a 'natural' spread of flowers later.

"He could be very imaginative in his planting techniques, and once fired plant seeds at a cliff face from a shotgun to give a 'natural' spread of flowers."

THE UNDERGROUND EMERGENCY SERVICE

An unassuming, plain, grey building, next door to the New Inn in Clapham, is something of a shrine in caving circles. It was once a pub, then stables for the inn next door, but now is known simply as the CRO Depot, which stands for Cave Rescue Organisation. It possesses such a generic title because, like the FA Cup, it was the first of its kind in the world, and didn't need a name to distinguish it from other cave rescue teams – there weren't any. Since its formation in 1935, the CRO has rescued nearly 3,000 unfortunate folk, many from underground, but also walkers and climbers on the surface, as the organisation doubles as a mountain rescue team.

The modern CRO is a large and very professional organisation, but amazingly, all 80 team members are volunteers and the whole operation is funded by donations.

The estate charges a nominal fee to follow the **Reginald Farrer Nature Trail** along the main Ingleborough track, although it is more of a landscaped garden stroll, and a free bridleway alternative runs parallel, to the cave and beyond.

Estate connections apart, a good deal else to see in Clapham can easily fill half a day. An excellent guide for pottering around the village is the free map/leaflet produced by the village development association (www.claphamyorkshire.co.uk) and found in all the shops and cafés. It shows where little St James Church is hidden away in the trees; how to find the village hall that often has displays of local artists; and exactly where the five bridges over the beck are. Interestingly, two buildings in the village not featured on the map as they are not open to visitors, but which locals are very proud of hosting, are The *Dalesman* magazine, bastion of Slow principles, which has offices in a small cottage near the village hall, and the headquarters of the **Cave Rescue Organisation**, the building next to the pub (see above).

¶¶ FOOD & DRINK

Growing with Grace Station Rd, LA2 8ER ☎ 01524 251723 ⬧ www.growingwithgrace. org.uk. A Quaker co-operative organic farm shop selling a wide variety of vegetables, fruit and whole foods. Closed Sun and Mon.

New Inn Hotel Old Rd ☎ 01524 251203 ⬧ www.newinn-clapham.co.uk. A large 18th-century coaching inn opposite the market cross. Two bars with open fires serving Yorkshire real ales. Main bar has a collection of caving cartoons by Jim Eyre, one of the local early cave explorers.

The Old Manor Bunkhouse Church Av ☎ 01524 251144 🖰 www.claphambunk.com. Not just cheap and cheerful accommodation in Clapham, but the only bunkhouse in the country with a bar to have featured in CAMRA's Good Beer Guide. Food at weekends.

SHOPPING & ACTIVITIES

Beckside Yarns & Needlecrafts Beckside Gallery, Church Av ☎ 01524 251122 🖰 www.becksideyarns.co.uk. A shop celebrating the local tradition of wool knitting. A wide variety of yarns for sale.

Ingleborough Hall LA2 8EF ☎ 01524 251265 🖰 www.ingleboro.co.uk. Run by Bradford Metropolitan District Council as an outdoor education centre, primarily for Bradford schoolchildren, but they do offer day and half-day activities for non-residents in expert-led climbing, caving and gorge scrambling.

3 INGLEBOROUGH CAVE & GAPING GILL

☎ 01524 251242 🖰 www.ingleboroughcave.co.uk.

The entrance to the cave is a very obvious large hole in the side of the Clapham Beck valley, just over a mile upstream from Clapham village, so to say the cavern was discovered in 1837 would be stretching the truth. The cave's existence had been known to locals for hundreds of years, but the 19th-century's upsurge in both scientific exploration and commercial development prompted the estate to blast away a rubble barrier a short way into the chamber. What they found beyond turned out to be a link to one of the most extensive cave systems in Britain, and a goldmine for their fledgling tourist industry.

"The cave is now fully lit throughout and hard hats are compulsory, but 40 or so years ago visitors were advised to 'mind their heads' and were given individual candles to light their way."

Thousands of visitors have enjoyed the guided tour in the subsequent 170 years. Visitor numbers to Ingleborough Cave reached their peak in the 1960s when the health and safety culture was not quite as obsessive as today. The cave is now fully lit throughout and hard hats are compulsory, but 40 or so years ago visitors were advised to 'mind their heads' and were given individual candles to light their way. Alan, one of the cave guides, was telling me of an entertaining recent visit from a deceptively harmless-seeming elderly couple. 'We've actually been here once before,' the old gentleman said. 'Back in 1961 or 62 when we were both teenagers. I'm afraid we didn't behave

MY DESCENT INTO GAPING GILL

The karabiner clicked. 'Sit right back and keep your feet in,' my minder instructed, then he looked me in the eye, 'Okay, you ready? Away you go.' With that, a trap door opened and my chair disappeared down into absolute blackness with me in it, clutching to my midriff the items on Chester's list.

I'd been talking to Chester the night before in the bar of the New Inn in Clapham about my morning descent into Gaping Gill. 'You'll love it, it's a great experience but take something warm and waterproof,' he said. 'Too many people turn up at the winch in shorts, and bikinis even, not realising just where they are going. They treat it as a funfair ride – but it's a bit more than that. A head torch will be useful and a bit of food if you're planning on staying down a while. A roll-up keeps me warm enough but some folk like to have a small flask of coffee.' About ten seconds into the descent was the first of the several times that I was glad of Chester's advice. The pot-holing club members above had temporarily diverted the beck that created the main shaft, away from it, but there was still a fair amount of water around and I got well sprayed. Gaping Gill is a little like an inverted funnel in shape, so after the initial narrow entrance, although I couldn't see it, I could feel I was in a huge space – large enough to contain York Minster it turns out. It was a vulnerable feeling to be suspended in the middle of that with just tiny lights visible on the floor below and the roar of the waterfall echoing around the chamber. Almost before I knew it the chair came to a halt at the cave floor and I was helped out and moved to somewhere slightly drier to watch Kevin, the next descender, join us. 'God, did I just do that?' I thought as the chair hurtled out of the dark spray and into the dim light where we were.

The two of us had a brief tour from another club member and were then let loose to explore with head torches (cheers, Chester). Twenty minutes later, with more and more people arriving, and queuing for the chair out becoming a possibility, I went back up. Chester had said that the ascent would be different and it was. 'You'll see more 'cos your eyes are acclimatised to the dark; look out for Colley's ledge.' This is as far as Colley, the first caver to brave the descent, reached. He looked down into the black, couldn't see the floor and declared Gaping Gill bottomless. What Chester didn't tell me was that for some reason it's a lot wetter going back up.

I stepped out of the chair at the top, completely drenched and in a daze, handed in my numbered wristband (it's handy for them to know how many are still down there) and went to the checking-in tent to thank the team. I had, and still have, a real feeling of gratitude towards everyone in the Craven Pothole Club for enabling me to have such a privileged experience. It took the direct involvement of eight people to get me down and back: two doing the checking in, a winch man, a top chair man, two bottom chair men, a guide and an overseer. All were volunteers here on holiday and what did I pay? Ten pounds – a bargain. Long may it continue.

particularly well. I wrote my initials on the cave ceiling in candle soot, and my wife set fire to the person in front of her with her candle. It was an accident I think.' Alan pointed out the offending graffiti, which were still there after nearly 50 years.

For a reasonable fee, the guides, mostly serious ex-cavers themselves, provide a friendly and informative tour, taking about 50 minutes to travel a third of a mile in and returning the same way. The cave is dry, the paths level-ish and the only discomfort a bit of stooping here and there … not at all the claustrophobic experience you might expect.

If you do want a truly adrenalin-charged underground experience, you need not look much further. A mile uphill from Ingleborough Cave, following the dry valley of Trow Gill, you come to an area of 'pot holes' and 'shake holes', one of which warrants a safety fence around it. This is **Gaping Gill**, a slightly ominous name for something genuinely awe-inspiring.

Fell Beck, tumbling down the eastern side of Ingleborough thousands of years ago, found itself a crack in the soluble limestone to disappear down. Over the millennia this crack has widened into the largest cave chamber in Britain and Fell Beck's freefall descent into it forms the highest waterfall in the country, albeit not seen by many people. Sadly more than a few careless people eager for a closer look have made a quick and fatal descent, 365 feet to the floor of Gaping Gill, so take care near the edge.

"Fell Beck, tumbling down the eastern side of Ingleborough thousands of years ago, found itself a crack in the soluble limestone to disappear down."

The great news is that a much slower descent of Gaping Gill is possible, but only on two weeks of the year, the week of Whitsun Bank Holiday and the week leading up to August Bank Holiday. Local caving clubs set up a winch to lower willing members of the public down to the bottom of the cave and back for a nominal fee. Bradford Potholing Club run it in May (✆ 01484 683260 ⌂ www.bpc-cave.org.uk) and Craven Pothole Club in August (⌂ www.cravenpotholeclub.org). There must be a catch, I hear you say, and there is. So popular is this service that the wait for your turn at the top can be five hours at busy times. What you can do is put your name down then walk up nearby Ingleborough until it's time for your turn.

4 INGLETON

Ingleton is most definitely a town, albeit a small and friendly one, and it is a town that has very successfully reinvented itself after the collapse of a busy industrial past. The last of the coal mines closed in the 1930s, limestone quarrying stopped ten years later and the town lost its rail link courtesy of Dr Beeching in 1967. Most folk would agree that Ingleton has benefited from the first two changes, but not the last one: a locomotive in full steam, crossing the town viaduct on its way to Kirkby Lonsdale, would be an inspiring sight today.

Ingleton is thriving now because of tourism, with most visitors using it as a service base to explore the scenic delights of its hinterland. The nearest sample of this beautiful countryside is right on the doorstep, the **Ingleton Waterfalls Trail** (see page 32). This is one of two walks (the Reginald Farrer Nature Trail near Clapham being the other), where a fee is charged by the landowner for the privilege. I'm not madly keen on the principle of paying to walk, but I'll bite the bullet, since it's such a spectacular path. If you have found yourself here on a lousy weather day, or you're just feeling lazy, indoor diversions in Ingleton – a smattering of arts and craft shops, the pottery being the best, a few tea shops and four pubs – could be your option. Two of the cafés, Bernies and Inglesport, have an interesting history; next door to each other, Bernies was a café and Inglesport a caving equipment shop. When Inglesport started selling food and drink, the café next door replied by selling caving gear and they now exist in a state of healthy rivalry.

"If you have found yourself here on a lousy weather day, or you're just feeling lazy, indoor diversions in Ingleton could be your option."

Inglesport also operates **Ingleton's indoor climbing wall** (Main St ☎ 01524 241146 www.inglesport.com), which is available for experienced climbers. If you aren't, but would like to have a go anyway, then ask in the shop about freelance instructors who can coach on the wall, or even take you down a cave.

Ingleton is one of the few places hereabouts to boast a heated **outdoor pool** (☎ 01524 241147 www.ingletonpool.co.uk; open in summer), which you can find down by the riverside behind the church. The pool was built by striking coal miners in the 1930s, at the height of the lido boom.

You could also take a country lane stroll half a mile past the pool to the tiny village of **Thornton in Lonsdale**. Sir Arthur Conan Doyle was married

Ingleton Waterfalls Trail
❋ OS Explorer map OL2; start: Falls Café, grid reference SD693732.

This 4½-mile walk is a little classic. The walkers' oracle Alfred Wainwright himself declared: 'Surely, of its kind, this is the most delightful walk in the country. And not only delightful; it is interesting, exciting, captivating and, in places, awesome.' The trail is well signposted in Ingleton and starts down in the valley bottom where the Thornton road crosses two small rivers, just above their confluence to form the embryonic River Greta. If you are in a car it is worth parking down here by the café rather than up in town, as your walk entrance fee includes parking.

Traditionally the route is clockwise ascending the valley of the River Twiss first; do not be tempted to go maverick, starting with the River Doe and travelling anti-clockwise. You may think that you are avoiding the crowds (and the fee) but in reality you will meet everybody else travelling in the opposite direction at some point, probably on all the steep and narrow staircase sections! For solitude, and that would always be my choice on a walk as beautiful as this, the advice is go early. Last time I visited, the nice man in the ticket office said, 'We officially open at 09.00 and I couldn't possibly condone anyone setting off before then as they would not be covered by the owner's insurance (said with a twinkle in his eye). In any case, it never gets busy until about 11.00 . . . lazy lot these trippers.' Another alternative recommended by Wainwright, who was a confirmed sociopath, is to do the walk in winter when there are no crowds and the falls are either roaring with flood water or festooned with ice sculptures.

As soon as you enter the limestone gorge of Swilla Glen near the start of the walk, it becomes obvious why this area is deemed so special, Natural England designating it as a Site of Special

in St Oswald's Church here and celebrated afterwards in the Marton Arms opposite. You would do well to emulate him as it is a great old pub, but mind your behaviour, as the old village stocks are still fully functional nearby.

⊪ FOOD & DRINK

Bernies Café Main St ✆ 01524 241802 🖰 www.berniescafe.co.uk. Basic hearty nosh surrounded by cavers and bikers. Also sells outdoor gear.

Ingleborough Limestone Beef Whaitber Farm, Westhouse LA6 3PQ ✆ 01524 241442. Meat reared on the high fell, sold from the farm when available.

Marton Arms Thornton in Lonsdale ✆ 01524 241281 🖰 www.themartonarms.co.uk. The building dates from the 13th century and retains a lot of its old charm. For drinkers this is an exceptional place with many local cask ales, beers and ciders available, and over 200 malt whiskies to choose from. Food is also highly regarded.

Scientific Interest (SSSI) for its geology alone. The fenced path clings to the valley side as it passes through a tunnel of overhanging ash and hazel boughs on its way to Manor Bridge and the first of the cascades, **Pecca Falls**, as it leaps over a hard band of greywacke rock. In the next 500 yards the river tumbles over seven rock steps at **Pecca Twin Falls**, **Hollybush Spout**, other nameless rapids and finally, **Thornton Force**, at 46 feet the highest of them all. This time the hard ledge is limestone and the soft rock beneath is vertically folded slate.

For the laid-back and sedate, this is the ideal spot for a laze and/or picnic, while the bold and restless members of the party brave the slippery walk behind the falls or swim in the plunge pool itself. Not far above Thornton Force, the route leaves the Twiss Valley to contour around the hill on the very old Twisleton Lane track and reaches a high point of 934 feet above sea level before joining the valley of the **River Doe** for the descent.

Beezley Falls marks the start of the most dramatic section of the whole walk, and is closely followed by **Rival Falls** and the dark depths of **Baxengill Gorge**. The inaccessible nature of this place has left the woods relatively undisturbed to form one of the best remnants of ancient semi-natural forest in the area. The giant mature oaks, rare mosses and liverworts, and nesting pied flycatchers and redstarts are in the care of the Woodland Trust, who own and manage this part of the valley.

Snow Falls is one of the last spectacular diversions on view, before the path passes through an old limestone quarry and back into Ingleton.

🖑 www.ingletonwaterfallstrail.co.uk

Ingleton Pottery Under the viaduct ✆ 01524 241363 🖑 www.ingletonpottery.co.uk. An old Unsworth family business. You can watch stoneware pottery being hand thrown and buy the results.

5 WHITE SCAR CAVE

6255 Hawes Rd, LA6 3AW ✆ 01524 241244 🖑 www.whitescarcave.co.uk; open Feb–Oct daily, plus weekends in winter (weather permitting).

North of Ingleton, Twisleton Dale carries the main road to Hawes, past White Scar Cave and through the little hamlet of Chapel le Dale. The White Scar experience is very different to that of Ingleborough Cave. It is the longest show cave in Britain so at 80 minutes the tour lasts longer. The beck that created Ingleborough Cave has moved to a lower system leaving the show cave dry, whereas White Scar is an active cave with the noise and moisture of its creative beck still very much in evidence, meaning there's a real risk of the cave closing in very wet weather.

There is car parking at the cave entrance, a shop and a well appointed café; you can even have a virtual tour of the cave on the new website without leaving home. The White Scar experience is convenient, modern and slick, but I have to admit I prefer the 'slower' experience of Ingleborough Cave.

6 KINGSDALE

By car, the way to Kingsdale is a narrow, poorly signposted minor road that sets off from Ingleton in the wrong direction entirely, then doubles back at Thornton in Lonsdale if you follow the sign for 'Dent'. Up a steep hill, down another one, round a bend and suddenly there it is; a hidden valley, tiny and tucked away. This is one of Wainwright's 'shyly hidden places' where 'life here is as it should be; two farmsteads the only habitation, animals graze undisturbed and birds enjoy sanctuary.'

"Kingsdale is just a great place to be, an almost guaranteed deserted oasis for those that need solitude to wander."

Kingsdale is just a great place to be, an almost guaranteed deserted oasis for those that need solitude to wander, which was why I was surprised on a visit in May 2009 to see what looked like an impromptu campsite near the head of the valley. I assumed that it was a meet of the caving fraternity but on closer investigation found myself in the middle of an archaeological excavation. The group conducting the dig were from the local Ingleborough Archaeology Group and one of their number, Dave Johnson, kindly showed me around the site.

'In 2006 we were excavating a known medieval building when we found remains of a fire pit which was dated to between 6960 and 6660BC, putting it within the Mesolithic (or Middle Stone Age) period,' he explained. 'What we're doing now is concentrating on features to the side of the fire pit that may be remains of post-holes for a temporary shelter used maybe by hunters, foragers or chert knappers.' (Chert is the limestone equivalent of flints in chalk, I learnt from Dave.) The group offers the opportunity for volunteers to join their number, be trained up in a variety of techniques and assist on digs. Contact them if you are interested in future projects (✆ 01524 271072 ☞ www. ingleborougharchaeologygroup.org.uk).

When I chanced upon the archaeologists, I was on my way to a place in Kingsdale that, in Victorian times, was quite a tourist draw. **Yordas Cave** was once a show cave with an admission fee but is now a little-visited hole in the hillside. An inscribed date of 1653 on one of the internal walls testifies to how long this place has been known about, indeed the name indicates an even older heritage. Yordas was a legendary Norse giant who would lure boys into the depths and devour them. Putting aside the dangers of being eaten by Vikings, Yordas is considered one of the safer caves to enter without a guide or specialist equipment, although in today's paranoid health-and-safety culture the British Caving Association would probably never put that in writing. Although not signposted it is marked on the OS map and is relatively easy to find. Just before the last building in the dale where the road is gated is a wooded dry valley. Beyond the low entrance a torch is all that is needed, and the bigger the better, to see your footing and the details of the roof formations 60 feet above. At the back of the cave, 30 yards from the entrance, Yordas Gill flows across the floor from right to left, having fallen in through the roof as an elegant waterfall. This is a great place for sensible freelance exploration but not after very wet weather when the cave floor can flood and be very muddy afterwards.

"Putting aside the dangers of being eaten by Vikings, Yordas is considered one of the safer caves to enter without a guide or specialist equipment."

On the fell-side above Yordas Wood, just below the summit of Gragareth, lies an area referred to on the map as Turbary Pasture. Turbary is the ancient commoners' right to collect turf or peat, and the fuel was transported via the Turbary Road which is present as a track and makes an excellent terrace walk or cycle along the side of Kingsdale.

7 CHAPEL LE DALE

🏠 **Old Hill Inn** (see pages 36 and 173)

A church, a pub and some caves; that is just about it for Chapel le Dale, but the church is delightful, the pub magnificent and the caves have intriguingly weird names.

This hamlet is named after 'the church in the valley', **St Leonard's**, a tiny 17th-century building with a history intrinsically linked to the railway that crosses the head of the dale. The church is made of local limestone. On the west wall of the nave is a black Dent marble memorial which reads:

> To the memory of those who through accidents, lost their
> lives, in constructing the railway works, between Settle and
> Dent Head. This tablet was erected at the joint expense, of
> their fellow workmen and the Midland Railway Company
> 1869 to 1876.

The railway company obviously felt some small responsibility for these accidental deaths as it paid for an extension to the graveyard (hardly a gesture that would have earned them an 'Investors in People' logo today) – but not for the many more that perished from smallpox or fights; some of those victims lie in unmarked graves here.

My recommended slow route linking Chapel le Dale with Ingleton is not the busy main road but the old Roman road on the other side of Twisleton Dale. It is a pleasant drive and an even better cycle, quiet and relatively flat until Meal Bank at Ingleton. This route can be extended into a circular easy walk, or a more testing bike ride, on the bridleway over Twisleton Fell. Big plusses are that you get to pass the wonderfully named **Hurtle Pot** and **Jingle Pot** caves near the church, and cross the fantastic limestone pavement on the fell top. The only minus, except for pushing your bike up or down the steep bits, are the unrestricted views of the still-operating Ingleton quarry – a real eyesore.

Old Hill Inn

Chapel le Dale LA6 3AR ☎ 01524 241256 ⌨ www.oldhillinn.co.uk.

By far the most visited building in Chapel le Dale is the Old Hill Inn. Although it started its long life as a farm in 1650, this building has been a pub of repute, and sometimes ill repute, for a long time. Sheep drovers were their main customers in the 17th and 18th centuries but in the late 1800s, railway building time, the pub was more like a Wild West saloon with 6,000 navvies needing to be watered and entertained. Last century quieter times returned, with hill-walkers and cavers the main clientele … and the occasional celebrity visitor; Winston Churchill was a regular when visiting the Dales.

The 1970s and 80s saw a brief return to the wild old days when the Old Hill became a very basic boozer but an extremely popular one. I have many very fond memories of a misspent youth here: some wild and long Saturday nights in a bar packed with cavers and walkers. Things were very informal; one of the bar games was cavers attempting to squeeze through the spokes of an old cartwheel, the bar staff wore wellies to cope with the quantity of beer on the floor and most of the customers staggered out to their tents in the garden in the early hours of the morning. Those days are long gone and the Old Hill is much more sedate now; some would say it has lost a lot of its character but one thing is for certain, the quality of the beer and food is higher than it has ever been.

The Old Hill Inn does handy accommodation either as B&B in the pub or on its own small touring caravan site – see *Accommodation*, page 173.

THE CUMBRIAN CORNER

The minor road that heads up Kingsdale from Ingleton sneaks right over the shoulder of the biggest of the Three Peaks, Whernside. At its highest point it does something very strange; as it starts to drop down steeply into Deepdale, and towards **Dentdale**, it stays within the Yorkshire Dales National Park, but leaves the county of North Yorkshire. Since 1974 this valley down to **Sedbergh** and the parallel valley of **Garsdale** to the north have been part of Cumbria, but you try telling the local farmers that they are not Yorkshiremen if you dare!

Half of the range of hills beyond Sedbergh is also part of the national park and I have therefore included them. The **Howgills** are hills apart; distinctly neither the Pennines nor the Cumbrian Fells but rubbing shoulders with both.

8 SEDBERGH
🏠 **Lock Bank Farm** (see page 173)
⛺ **Holme Farm** (see page 173)

The little-known River Rawthey squeezes its way between the Pennine hills of the Yorkshire Dales and the Howgill Fells just to their west. On its northern bank, just before it spills into the grand River Lune, sits Sedbergh, a market town with a castle mound and venerable bowed buildings lining a cobbled main street. Sedbergh is a very self-contained little place, comfortable in its own skin, which until recently was really only known to walkers or mountain bikers with designs on the southern Howgills, or those with connections to the

"Sedbergh is a very self-contained little place, comfortable in its own skin."

prestigious private school whose buildings dominate the land between the main street and the river. **Sedbergh School**, founded in 1525, has by necessity moved with the times and now has modern facilities, day pupils and a significant proportion of girl students. Thirty-five years ago, when I was a schoolboy myself and visiting Sedbergh on a school trip, things were far more traditional. The male-only boarders were ripe for our astonished ridicule as we leant over the school wall and saw the 'posh kids' all in shorts … right up to 18-year-old sixth-formers!

These days mention the name Sedbergh and many people will think of books, because this is officially England's **book town** and partner to Hay-on-Wye in Wales (where it all started) and Wigtown in Scotland. The town's re-branding has been brilliantly orchestrated by a group of local residents who realised after the 2001 foot-and-mouth disease outbreak how vulnerable rural communities dependent on farming were. 'This has been so good for the town,' said Carol Nelson, manager of the project. 'It's brought more people in, which supports and safeguards the future of the shops that really matter – the butcher, grocer, hardware shop, post office and the like – but it also allows us to celebrate the glory of books. The sort of books people buy in a book town aren't your throwaway airport novellas, but important ones that you are prepared to keep, read to your children and which eventually become old friends.' It's not just literature that is thriving here either; the town has a really active music scene with its own brass band, choral society, orchestra and biennial music festival in June.

Quakers in Sedbergh

Less well known than its contribution to books is Sedbergh's importance in the beginnings of the Quaker movement. In 1652, George Fox, the founder of the Society of Friends, preached in and around the town to hundreds of local folk. His sermon from a rock on Firbank Fell, now known as Fox's Pulpit, is widely held to be the founding moment of the Society. Twenty two years after these events local 'Friends' built a meeting house at **Briggflats** by the river half a mile west of Sedbergh. It has survived the intervening 400 years as the oldest meeting house in the north of England, its plain, wood-bench-simplicity, testimony to the 'Slow' and minimalist Friends' philosophy. Briggflats is only a mile's stroll away from Sedbergh town centre along the riverside Dales Way, with a seat in the peaceful burial ground the ideal spot for a moment of meditation before the return path across the fields.

Farfield Mill

Garsdale Rd, LA10 5LW ℡ 01539 621958 🖥 www.farfieldmill.org.

As in many other parts of the country, the local Quaker movement was associated with Victorian industry, and in the mid 19th century Sedbergh boasted five water-powered woollen mills. The best preserved of these by a long way is Farfield Mill, just east of Sedbergh on the way to Garsdale.

For years, Joseph Dover toiled away as manager of Hepplethwaite Mill, to the west of Sedbergh, dreaming of owning his own mill. Finally, in 1836 he had saved the necessary £490 to buy land at Farfield on a bend of the River Clough, and start construction. A year after the mill was completed, Joseph died but his two sons developed the business into a lucrative concern that remained within the Dover family for 100 years.

The mill ceased operating in 1992 and was subsequently renovated by the Sedbergh and District Buildings Preservation Trust. It now operates as a multi-use venue – part weaving museum and part 'Slow' shopping mall, selling books, art and craft work, and lots of textiley things. You can sign up for weaving workshops or just bring your own knitting to the café and join the 'knit and natter' group, while the kids go off on a treasure hunt. A great place to spend a wet afternoon, and worth the small entrance fee.

🍴 FOOD & DRINK

Green Door Sweet Shop Main St ℡ 01539 620089 🖥 www.thegreendoorshop.co.uk. Do you ever yearn for the nostalgic taste of pear drops, Pontefract cakes and sherbet lemons? Then enter the Green Door because they are all here, with hundreds more besides.

Howgill Fellside Ice Cream Lock Bank Farm, Howgill ℡ 01539 620252 🖥 http:/ dareswayluxuryices.co.uk. Ice creams and sorbets made on-site at the farm using milk from their own herd. Mouthwatering flavours include liquorice and blackcurrant and vodka lemon meringue. Also has self-catering cottage to sleep eight (See *Accommodation*, page 173).

The Sedbergh Café Main St ℡ 01539 621389 🖥 www.thesedberghcafe.com. An Edwardian-style gem, serving a wide range of tea and filter coffees from Taylors of Harrogate, and top-quality snacks. Gift and food shop attached.

BOOKSHOPS

Sedbergh's five book-town shops are:

Dales and Lakes Book Centre 72 Main St ℡ 01539 620125 🖥 www.sedbergh.org.uk/ booktown/dlbc.html. Mainly local interest and guidebooks; this place doubles as the tourist information centre.

Patch and Fettle 77 Main St ✆ 07967 422873 ⌂ www.patchandfettle.co.uk. Describes itself as a 'tiny shop of delights'.

RFG Holletts and Son 6 Finkle St ✆ 01539 620298 ⌂ www.holletts-rarebooks.co.uk. A specialist antiquarian bookshop open by appointment.

Sleepy Elephant 41 Main St ✆ 01539 621770 ⌂ www.sleepyelephant.co.uk. A wide range of books including scarce books on art design.

Westwood Books Leisure House, Long Lane ✆ 01539 621233 ⌂ www.westwoodbooks. co.uk. A very large stock of new, secondhand and antiquarian books on all subjects.

9 THE HOWGILL FELLS

⌂ **Cross Keys Inn** Cautley (see page 172)

The Howgills are a very discrete range of hills, geologically separate from the Yorkshire Dales, and with the River Lune (and more obviously the M6 motorway) providing the boundary with the mountains of the Lake District.

Such is the gentle rounded aspect of these hills from a distance that a friend of mine once likened them to a giant plate of dumplings. Alfred Wainwright was less obsessed with food, and in his book *Walks on the Howgill Fells* preferred the metaphor 'a huddle of squatting elephants'. This is very different country, and what makes it so is an absence of things rather than a list of attributes: no roads or buildings, virtually no trees except in the deepest creases and, most striking of all, no walls – not a single one. This makes for a particularly liberating place to walk in, as you can genuinely just wander where you fancy, terrain permitting – and make no mistake, despite the distant gentle impressions, some serious gradients lie hidden away.

> "Such is the gentle rounded aspect of these hills from a distance that a friend of mine once likened them to a giant plate of dumplings."

The most accessible Howgill is most definitely **Winder**, a mere morning stroll from Sedbergh, albeit a very steep one, but longer treks allow you to lose yourself in this special place. For a nice, easy stroll into the heart of the Howgills without too much climbing, the walk along the beck from near the Cross Keys to **Cautley Spout waterfall** is highly recommended. The ascent of the Howgills' highest point, **The Calf** (2,220 feet), via Cautley Spout waterfall and then down to Sedbergh makes a fine day's walk, but the plum route for me is **Black Force** via **Carlingill Beck**.

THE RETURN OF THE PEREGRINE FALCON

Back in the late 1970s, when I was still in my teens, I read a book called *The Peregrine* by J A Baker, a man obsessed by these most magnificent of birds. For this passionate and poetic naturalist, peregrines didn't just fly, they sliced a parabola in a smooth outpouring, like water gliding over stone, or fell as a black bill-hook does into splinters of white wood. What's more, his meticulously observed winter's diary wasn't only inspirational prose, but damned good science too.

Some of his passion rubbed off on me and I dreamt of seeing peregrine falcons flying in the wild. Those were dark days for birds of prey generally; organo-chlorine pesticides added to crop seeds had found their way into the food chain via seed-eating birds and had ended up in such concentrations in the bodies of top predators that the poisoning proved fatal. Where it did not actually kill the birds, it weakened eggshells to the point where they smashed easily in the nest and breeding failed. By the 1970s the peregrine was on the brink of extinction in England. Those few pairs that did nest on isolated crags in the north and west of the country were guarded 24 hours a day by dedicated volunteers to prevent the theft of their rare eggs or chicks. Thirty years ago egg-collecting was far more widely practised than today, and the hatched young birds could be sold to unscrupulous falconers for thousands of pounds.

I was introduced to my first pair of wild peregrines by an inspirational schoolteacher, Alan Stoddart, who, when on holiday from teaching me and my peers in industrial Lancashire, lived in a caravan in Dentdale. The nest, or eyrie, was on a crag called Combe Scar near the village of Dent, and one Easter I and a few other equally excited schoolboys were sworn to secrecy and taken up to meet the 'guard' in a derelict barn below the crag.

For the following hour or two we watched entranced through binoculars as the male (tiercel) screamed into view at a speed scarcely believable, to deliver food to the female (falcon) who sat incubating eggs on the nest, their staccato calls echoing around the combe. I have seen peregrines many times since, but nothing has ever matched that first electric experience.

Thankfully, those poisonous pesticides have long since been banned, and wildlife crime is now very well policed. Consequently peregrine falcons have made a remarkable recovery all over the country, recolonising all their old haunts and even spreading on to the artificial cliffs (tall buildings) in many towns and cities. The Yorkshire Dales now boast about twenty pairs nesting on crags dotted across the national park, including, I am happy to note, the descendants of 'my' pair, still on Combe Scar.

You could come across them anywhere in the Dales, usually given away by their distinctive anchor shape in flight, like a squat kestrel, or their phenomenal hunting speed of over 100mph, if you are fortunate enough to see it. For an almost guaranteed viewing though, go to Malham Cove where the RSPB has a telescope set up between Easter and August on the resident peregrine nest.

Unfortunately it starts with a six-mile drive/taxi ride/hitched lift on the minor road from Sedbergh, through the hamlet of Howgill to Carlingill Bridge (OS Explorer map OL19; ❋ grid reference SD624996). But within minutes of starting, the M6 is out of sight and your only company is grazing dales ponies, wheatears protesting loudly from boulder-tops, and dippers feeding by (and in) the water. You are forced to criss-cross the beck as the valley walls close in (it may be impassable after heavy rain) and finally reach the spot of the day, where Black Force Beck tumbles down its ravine to join you. Scan the skyline for ravens and peregrine falcons. Both routes to the tops involve some serious scrambling, up the side of either Black Force or Carlingill Beck and then you are back on gentle grassy slopes again. The route from there is your choice; back to the car via Uldale Head or Linghaw (three miles in total), or over some elephants' backs (Bush Howe and The Calf) to Sedbergh (seven miles in all).

¶¶ FOOD & DRINK

Cross Keys Inn Cautley LA10 5NE ✆ 01539 620284 ◌ www.cautleyspout.co.uk. A 400-year-old building that looks its age. Delicious rustic meals (rabbit pie with black pudding and bacon is the best seller). Alcohol is not for sale but you can bring your own for free (the pub has been unlicensed since 1902 and has the status of a temperance inn; the present tenant is a Quaker). Usefully placed for walks to Cautley Spout waterfall and also recommended for B&B (see *Accommodation* page 172).

10 DENTDALE

Whenever I arrive in Dentdale, and the sturdy little village that gives the valley its name, I always feel as if I'm coming home. This is no fanciful imagining brought on by the homely feel of the place, but because I did spend a fair proportion of my formative years here. Some inspired soul in my secondary school, in industrial Lancashire, decided that we 12-year-old 'townies' should experience country life, so the school bought a cottage in **Dent** for us to stay in. My weekend visits to White Hart House in the 1970s were a revelation; I discovered proper hills (Great Coum was my first summit), swam in clean rivers and saw the Milky Way in a clear, black, non-street-lit sky for the first time.

"Whenever I arrive in Dentdale, and the sturdy little village that gives the valley its name, I always feel as if I'm coming home."

A Dent walk
✤ OS Explorer map OL2; start: The Green, grid reference SD704869.

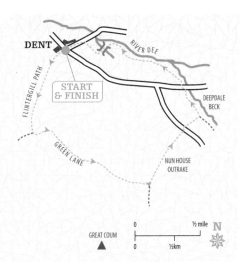

Most of Dent's visitors don't stray far from the main street, which isn't surprising as the cobbled surface and whitewashed cottage frontage give it a very attractive, almost Cornish fishing port, look. Also, this is where its two pubs, both cafés, the heritage centre and most of the shops are. I do, however, strongly recommend wandering a bit further afield, namely up the hillside at the back of the village along a lane called Flintergill. This route takes you past a stately Victorian building, formerly the Zion Chapel and now a meditation centre, open to all to just pop in for a moment's peace or join a more formal how-to-do-it course (⌂ www.meditationcentre.co.uk).

Where the tarmac lane becomes a bridleway (grid reference SD703867), you enter a Tolkienesque ravine – the real Flinter Gill that the road is named after. You may choose just to explore this enchanting place, or you can extend the walk in a variety of directions, and range of distances, on the maze of paths and bridleways on the valley side. My choice would be to continue up to join Green Lane, turn left and skirt the slopes of Great Coum for a mile (maybe detouring up the open access slopes to the summit), then descend Nun House Outrake. Back in the valley bottom, Deepdale Beck and the River Dee banks are the most entertaining routes back to Dent.

Times have changed, Dent is much busier now than it ever was in my youth, and sadly White Hart House was sold, but the village still retains its character and the dale remains many people's favourite.

The fact that it is a mere ten miles from Dent Head – where the Settle–Carlisle line calls in at **Dent Station** as it crosses the top of the valley – to Sedbergh where it meets the Rawthey Valley makes this quite a small dale, but one packed with fascinating detail. The River Dee is at the heart of much of it, especially in the upper dale, tumbling over limestone ledges, squeezing through narrow 'strids', and on numerous occasions playing hide and seek by disappearing underground, only to reappear hundreds of yards further downstream. The Dales Way footpath hugs the riverbank most of the way down, allowing views of the caves, which unusually abound down at valley-bottom level, and the rich and enchanting wildlife. You will probably see more dippers per mile of river here than anywhere else in Yorkshire.

11 AROUND DENT

🏠 **Bower Bank EcoBarn** Gawthrop (see page 173)

The fact that many locals still refer to this place as Dent Town gives us an inkling as to its importance in the past. In its heyday 200 years ago Dent had a market (where the George and Dragon now stands), a race course and managed to support 12 pubs and inns – venues of 'drunken riots, blasphemy, gambling quarrels and other bygone vices and follies' by all accounts. The industry that fuelled its economy was hand knitting, which was practised by just about everyone in the village; man, woman and child (see box below).

Dent's most famous son is undoubtedly **Adam Sedgwick**, who put his education in Dent Grammar School to good use by becoming professor of geology at Cambridge University, and was a personal friend of Queen Victoria and Prince Albert. His radical thinking in his field led him

THE TERRIBLE KNITTERS OF DENT

Peering through a Dent cottage window on an 18th-century winter's evening could reveal an eerie and disturbing sight. Ten or 12 adults, men and women, sit around the outside of the room, swaying their bodies in a circular motion in unison, and singing a rhythmic chant.

In the flickering candlelight, the shadows of their rapidly moving hands dance on the walls. Is this the meeting of a sinister religious cult? No, it's that of the Terrible Knitters of Dent.

'Terrible' referred not to the quality of their work but to the incredible speed with which they moved the wool and needles. They were paid on completed garments and a good knitter could start and finish a whole smock in a day. Every week, a cart would arrive from Farfield Mill in Sedbergh loaded with wool and would return full of completed garments – miner's jerseys, army stockings and caps, bump-caps for the slave colonies and high-quality woollens bound for the stores of London; they were all made in the parlours of Dentdale.

to being dubbed the father of English geology and prompted a water fountain enclosed in a block of Shap granite to be erected in his honour opposite the George and Dragon. It is probably the most photographed object in the village.

Behind Adam Sedgwick's fountain and down a short alley you will find the old, squat, grey stone **church of St Andrew**, surrounded by clipped yews and gravestones. As a boy I remember being morbidly fascinated by stories of a vampire's tomb here. In reality George Hodgson was a farmer who regularly drank sheep's blood as a tonic – it can't have done him much harm as he lived to 94, and his 'vampire' grave is in the church porch.

￦ FOOD & DRINK

Stone Close Tea Room Main St ☏ 01539 625231. Housed in a 17th-century listed building, this well-established tea room prides itself on the fresh, local, seasonal, organic, and fair trade credentials of its food and drink. All the baking is done by Diana on the premises.

SHOPPING

Hill Studio Main St ☏ 01539 625354 ⌂ www.johncooke.org. The studio of the nationally renowned artist John Cooke upstairs and the Best Cellars craft shop below.

Sophie's Wild Woollens The Shop on the Green ☏ 01539 625323. Sophie carries on the Terrible Knitters tradition. Lots of colourful modern designs all knitted locally.

12 DENT STATION

⌂ **Deeside House** (see page 173)

Dentdale, like neighbouring Garsdale, displays a typically Viking pattern of settlement – a scattering of farmsteads, with few if any villages. A cluster of buildings, near the top end of the dale, that don't quite manage to form a hamlet, are sometimes lumped together as Cowgill, but more often than not nowadays this corner is named after its most illustrious building.

Dent's railway station sets some kind of record for being further away from the place after which it is named than anywhere else in Britain – the village is a whopping four miles away.

Many people have been caught out, stepped off the train and then been faced with a yomp into town, but it's much worse the other way around. Walking from the village to the station is up a killer hill, as Dent Station holds another record: at 1,150 feet above sea level, it is the highest mainline station in England.

Most of the other buildings at this end of the dale are lower down, snuggled along the banks of the Dee, which is at its photogenic and playful best here. The whitewashed Sportsman's Inn sits in an enviable spot, with the chapel not far away, and a short mile upstream, a favourite spot of mine, is the old YHA building. Unfortunately, it's closed as a hostel now, but you can still stay there by hiring it as a private self-catering house (see page 173). Not far from the old youth hostel, at Stonehouse, the highly sought-after **Dent black marble** was quarried and polished. You can see it used decoratively in St Andrew's Church, Dent, and the Railway Memorial in St Leonard's in Chapel le Dale.

"The Dee is at its photogenic and playful best here."

Two **walks** here that I always enjoy are a stroll down the river to Ibberth Peril waterfall and back, and an ascent of Great Knoutberry Hill (possibly the best view in the Dales from the top) via Arten Gill.

13 GARSDALE

🏠 **Garsdale B&B** (see page 172)

This most northwesterly of the Yorkshire Dales holds the odd double distinction of being one of the most visited of the dales but the least known. The main road west out of busy Wensleydale snakes along the whole length of Garsdale, from top to bottom, but hundreds, sometimes thousands, of people a day pass through, on their way to scenic Wensleydale, or the wild and peaceful Howgills, unwittingly bypassing a landscape with all the same attributes in humble Garsdale. Key to this phenomenon is that there is no village in Garsdale to tempt visitors to stop, and few side roads to draw them off the A684, and slow them down.

RED SQUIRRELS

Garsdale is isolated enough to be one of the harassed red squirrel's few islands of refuge from its aggressive and disease-carrying cousin, the grey. This is one of 17 woodland areas in northern England where active management is taking place to help the beleaguered reds. Mature cone-bearing Scots pines and larches are encouraged instead of the oaks and hazels preferred by the greys, and any aliens that get in are trapped and killed – controversial but necessary.

Look out for ginger 'tufties' in Grisedale, Dodderham Moss above Dent station and Coat Weggs Woods near Garsdale church.

It takes a conscious effort to pause and explore here, but try it, because the rewards are rich. The two best opportunities are where minor roads leave the A684, one at Tom Croft Hill, only two miles from Sedbergh, which gives access to Rise Hill and footpaths following the gorgeous River Clough, and the other higher up the dale, the old road to Grisedale.

Grisedale is often labelled the 'Dale that Died' after a 1970s television programme of the same name which documented the last days of the farming families of the dale. It is a deserted place now but great walking country, especially since recent open access legislation has made the surrounding hills available for walkers. Both Wild Boar Fell here, and Rise Hill on the other side of the dale, are strangely devoid of public rights of way, so until open access they were no-go areas.

FOOD & DRINK

The Moorcock Inn Garsdale Head LA10 5PU ☎ 01969 667488 🖰 www.moorcockinn.com. A welcoming sight at a lonely moor-top crossroads. The inside environs may be rustic and the beer traditionally Yorkshire (Black Sheep and Copper Dragon), but the menu is extensive and imaginative with a continental twist.

RIBBLESDALE

The River Ribble does not spend much time in Yorkshire before it defects to Lancashire. A good way to see every inch of the valley is to follow the Ribble Way footpath which starts at the official source of the river, four miles northeast of the railway. Consequently, the place **Ribblehead**, where the much-photographed railway viaduct of the Settle–Carlisle line straddles Batty Moss, isn't actually the head of the valley, but let's not split hairs. The gloriously lazy way to see most of Upper Ribblesdale is to board the train at Ribblehead and rattle away south, with

"The gloriously lazy way to see most of Upper Ribblesdale is to board the train at Ribblehead and rattle away south."

Ingleborough filling the window on the starboard side and Pen-y-ghent likewise to port. They both come closest to the train and each other at **Horton in Ribblesdale**, the official start and finish of the Three Peaks Challenge. Six miles down the line at Settle, the railway and river both leave the national park and go their separate ways.

14 RIBBLEHEAD VIADUCT

To Network Rail this is the site of 'Bridge 66 and station'; to everyone else it is one of the most iconic railway landmarks in the world – the Ribblehead Viaduct. Over 400 yards long, 104 feet high and with 24 arches, it took 6,000 men to build, with 200 losing their lives in the process. To learn about the drama of the viaduct construction and its subsequent history you can visit the Ribblehead visitor centre in the station or get hold of a copy of *Thunder in the Mountains: The Men Who Built Ribblehead* by W R Mitchell. Now in his eighties, Bill, a former editor of the *Dalesman* magazine and self-confessed sufferer of the incurable disease of 'Settle and Carlisle-itis', has produced a riveting account of the soap opera goings-on at Ribblehead. Life in the shanty towns of Jerusalem and the Jerico, rat infestations in Belgravia, the doings of Welsh Jack and Nobby Scandalous, earthquakes, floods and murders – it's all covered.

The only other building at Ribblehead is its pub, **The Station Inn**, but scattered farmsteads appear as the Chapel le Dale and Horton roads drop down to less exposed climes. A short way down this latter route, and accessible on foot from the station, is **Ribblehead Quarry**, disused since 1999 and now being re-colonised by wildlife. The quarry is part of **Ingleborough National Nature Reserve** and a 1½-mile walking trail leads you around its waterfalls, ponds and rock gardens. You can pick up a leaflet from the station or download one from ⌕ www.naturalengland. org.uk. Look out for ravens, oystercatchers and ringed plover that breed here, but especially a small plant with five-pointed-star flowers; Yorkshire sandwort is one of the rarest plants in Britain and grows only here on Ingleborough, with its nearest relatives in Sweden.

"Look out for ravens, oystercatchers and ringed plover, but especially a small plant with five-pointed-star flowers; Yorkshire sandwort is one of the rarest plants in Britain."

Just beyond the quarry nature trail, **Colt Park Wood** is one tiny but exceptional part of the reserve. It has been described as the best example of an aboriginal scar limestone ash wood in the country, and the variety of exotic and scarce plants is astonishing. Visit in early summer and you could see globe flower, baneberry, alpine cinquefoil, yellow star of Bethlehem and the eccentrically named angular Solomon's seal.

🍴 FOOD & DRINK

The Station Inn Ribblehead LA6 3AS 📞 01524 241274 🖥 www.thestationinn.net.
This has always been a heart-warming sight for Three Peakers but on cold, wet days,
when the fire is roaring, it can be a life-saver. The best of the food is the traditional
English dishes of pies, mash and sausages, and the range of Yorkshire beers is impressive.
This is an atmospheric boozer but don't expect too much comfort. Bunk barn and
camping available.

FELL RUNNING

One question that has always intrigued me about fell runners is not where they do it, how they go so
fast, or even what the best technique is – but why they do it?

Peter Pozman, a 60-year-old teacher from near Wetherby, put me right. 'You know', he said, 'That's a question I ask myself every race, not long after the start, on the first uphill bit when me lungs are starting to scream. I'd always enjoyed walking up the fells, but the older I got the more I realised that I was running out of time to do them all, so I thought I'd better speed up a bit. By jogging, I found I was doing a whole afternoon's walks in less than an hour and seeing loads of countryside in the process. I was doing this once from Nidderdale, up a fell called Great Whernside, when I met someone near the top who looked at me and my tracksuit and trainers and said, "You must be a fell runner". Jokingly I said, "In my dreams I am", but then I thought, "Yeah, I like the sound of that, I am actually fell running her", and I started to take myself a bit more seriously, eventually actually entering some races.

One of my finest moments was finishing first in the Male 55 and Over class, in a race in the North York Moors, run by a bloke called Dave Parry from Commondale. I love Dave's races – they're really informal. There'd be 80 to 100 of us stood at the start and Dave would shout, "Right, well, it's been snowin' out there and it's startin' to melt, so it'll be real slippy. Last year someone in too much of a hurry took a bit of a tumble, so you might want to go bit easy – Go!" And off we went. It was really horrible but I think the conditions suited me; my hill craft as a walker, and understanding of rough ground kept me out of the freezing water, and my feet stayed relatively dry, while the elite athletes couldn't get going. Later in the Eskdale Inn at Castleton, I was watching other people get prizes, when Dave said, "M 55, winner Pete Pozman", and I thought, "Wey hey! Fantastic! Three bottles of wine and my name in print!"

I had my feet plonked firmly on the ground last week though, as I was struggling up a really steep slope, and a fella was keeping up with me walking. "So this is fell running", he said. "Is it hard?". "Yes", I gasped. "Especially when I have to talk to people like you at the same time."

15 HORTON IN RIBBLESDALE

The system of adding an address to a place name, like Skipton on Swale or Thornton in Craven, makes sense when there is another place nearby to confuse it with. Horton's 'in Ribblesdale' makes no sense, as it is the only one for miles, and the nearest is deep in Lancashire – and also in Ribblesdale!

Strange names apart, Horton has much in common with many Dales villages: two pubs, an old arched bridge over the river, a Norman church dedicated to the ubiquitous St Oswald, monastic rule in medieval times and later, a bad dose of the plague.

"Horton has much in common with many Dales villages: two pubs, an old arched bridge over the river, and a bad dose of the plague."

What singles Horton out today is the influence of outdoor pursuits such as caving (at nearby Alum, Hall and Hunt pots and the Long Churn system), cycling and, overwhelmingly, long-distance walking. The Pennine Way and Ribble Way converge here, but the Three Peaks Challenge is by far the most popular. This route was never really invented, it just sort of evolved and then was popularised by Alfred Wainwright's description of it in *Walks in Limestone Country*, and by the Pen-y-ghent café's 'Three Peaks of Yorkshire club'.

The fell-running race over much the same route has a more definite history. It was first run in 1954 with six runners starting, all from Lancashire, and only three finishing. In April 2009, the 55th race had a staggering line-up of 900 starters, with the fastest time an equally impressive 2 hours and 55 minutes, and this time a Yorkshireman won it.

⁋ FOOD & DRINK

Pen-y-ghent Café Horton BD24 0HE ☎ 01729 860333. This place unashamedly caters for outdoor types in need of carbohydrate and rehydration, so food is hearty and simple (excellent, huge vegetarian breakfasts) and tea comes in pints. Can be very busy, especially at weekends.

UPDATES WEBSITE

You can post your comments and recommendations, and read the latest feedback and updates from other readers online at www.bradtupdates.com/yorkshiredales.

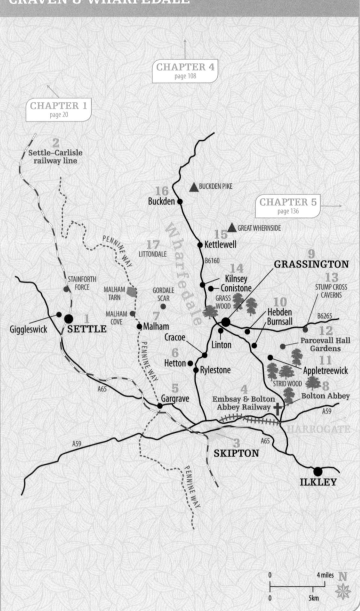

CHAPTER 4
page 108

CHAPTER 1
page 20

2
Settle–Carlisle
railway line

16
Buckden

BUCKDEN PIKE

CHAPTER 5
page 136

GREAT WHERNSIDE

15
Kettlewell

17
LITTONDALE

B6160

9
GRASSINGTON

13
STUMP CROSS
CAVERNS

STAINFORTH
FORCE

MALHAM
TARN

GORDALE
SCAR

14
Kilnsey
Conistone

GRASS
WOOD

10
Hebden
Burnsall

B6265

1
SETTLE

Giggleswick

MALHAM
COVE

7
Malham

Cracoe

Linton

12
Parcevall Hall
Gardens

6
Hetton

Rylestone

11
Appletreewick

STRID WOOD

8
Bolton Abbey

A65

5
Gargrave

4
Embsay & Bolton
Abbey Railway

A59

HARROGATE

A59

3
SKIPTON

A65

ILKLEY

PENNINE WAY

Wharfedale

0   4 miles
0   5km

N

52

2
CRAVEN & WHARFEDALE

This southernmost part of the Yorkshire Dales only just makes it into North Yorkshire, and its closeness to the big cities of Leeds and Bradford makes it probably the most visited region in the national park.

Three rivers drain south here: the Ribble, which then escapes westwards into Lancashire, the Aire, and the longest of the Dales watercourses, the Wharfe. Wharfedale's corridor-like nature sets it apart from the other Yorkshire Dales, that and the river that created it. If forced into a choice, I would have to plump for the **Wharfe** as my favourite Yorkshire river. Its deep, clear pools, strids, riffles and cascades provide unsurpassed variety of watery landscape, and arguably the richest wildlife in all of the national park.

Craven, the wild acres of high land to the west of Wharfedale, is a geological wonderland of all things limestone: pot-holes, 'clint and grike' pavements, disappearing rivers, collapsed caverns and amphitheatres – it's all here, and at its most spectacular around Malham.

SELF-POWERED TRAVEL
CYCLING

Road biking is biased towards the fit and experienced rider here purely because the only roads small and quiet enough to be pleasant on a bike tend to have really steep hills on them at some point. The Yorkshire Dales National Park's **Cycle the Dales scheme** (see page 10) has searched out some gentler routes termed as family rides, five of which fall into this region. They start at Settle, Skipton, Gargrave, Bolton Abbey and Grassington. My favourite of these, because it is a circuit that manages to keep off the main Wharfedale Road almost entirely, goes for 14 miles between Grassington, Conistone, Kettlewell, Hawkswick, Arncliffe and Kilnsey; join the route wherever.

For a longer day's ride with some testing hills but nothing gargantuan, try 29 miles of **Into Wharfedale**, a circuit taking in Skipton, Bolton Abbey and Grassington. For dedicated tourers, part of the Pennine Cycleway passes through here, and a fair chunk of the 130-mile Yorkshire Dales Cycleway, starting as it does in Skipton.

Off-road cycling is even less forgiving to the more leisurely rider than the local roads. No big forests with gentle tracks, or those nice, flat disused railway lines here. It's mainly fell-side tracks with serious inclines more suited to two-wheeled athletes. On the plus side, because this is well-drained limestone country, mud isn't generally a problem and many of the bridleways double as green lanes, so are fairly substantial. Again, the national park has a scheme that helps; **MTB the Dales** describes seven routes in Craven and Wharfedale, with a ten-mile Settle Loop being the least testing, and therefore the one for me. It crosses Langcliffe Scar and Ewe Moor, taking in the impressive Scaleber Force waterfall, and with only two short difficult sections punctuating a moderate ride. See the national parks website for details.

"Off-road cycling is even less forgiving to the more leisurely rider than the local roads."

Hopefully there will be one gentle alternative available soon. Off-road biking doesn't get any flatter than canal towpaths, and there are plans to extend the very popular Aire Valley Towpath Route on the Leeds and Liverpool Canal, from where it finishes now at Bingley, to Skipton. Watch this space.

CYCLE HIRE

Off the Rails Station Yard, Settle ✆ 01729 824419 ⌂ www.offtherails.org.uk. Daily adult bike hire, including tagalong, trailer and child seat.

HORSERIDING

If availability of trekking centres is a good measure, then this is the epicentre of horseriding in the whole of the Dales. Of the three centres in total, two are here.

If you bring your own horse then you, along with the mountain bikers, have access to the area's enormous mileage of bridleways, plus a new national trail primarily aimed at horse riders, the **Pennine Bridleway**, completed in 2012. Part of it, the Settle Loop (see above), is already open and well used. Accommodation for horses is available at **Craven Country Ride** (Pot Haw Farm, Coniston Cold ✆ 01756 749300 🖱 www. cravencountryride.co.uk).

RIDING CENTRES

Draughton Height Riding School Draughton, Skipton ✆ 01756 710242 🖱 www. draughtonridingcentre.com.
Kilnsey Trekking and Riding Centre Conistone ✆ 01756 752861 🖱 www.kilnseyriding.com.

WALKING

Two long-distance trails cross this region on a north/south line: the **Pennine Way** following the River Aire, and the **Dales Way** likewise but along the River Wharfe. Unless you are actually following either of these classic routes they are best avoided. More than enough alternative **day and half-day routes** exist with fewer people to share them with. My preferred strategy is to spread out the OS map (Explorer OL2 *Yorkshire Dales Southern & Western areas*) and plan my own, but there are many walking guides to do it for you if you prefer. The Harvey's *8 Walks Centred On* series has three maps for this area, all excellent: Settle, Skipton and Grassington. Two walks that don't make it on to any of these maps but are definitely in my hall of fame are Great Whernside from Kettlewell (see page 80) and a five-mile/three-pub crawl from Buckden, taking in Cray, Yockenthwaite, and the verdant hillside meadows above Hubberholme.

CRAVEN

While for the most part the individual dales of the Yorkshire Dales fit into easily identifiable chunks of scenery, the Craven district is a strangely nebulous idea with no neatly defined edges. I am taking it as stretching from the River Ribble in the west, handy as 'Ribble' means boundary in Anglo-Saxon, to the catchment of the Wharfe in the east. The small town of **Settle** sits along the east bank

"The Craven district is a strangely nebulous idea with no neatly defined edges."

of the Ribble with the frivolously named **Giggleswick** on the opposite side. Behind Settle the land rises steeply at the start of well over 100 square miles of wild upland dominated by carboniferous limestone.

i **TOURIST INFORMATION**

Grassington National Park Centre ☎ 01756 751690
Malham National Park Centre ☎ 01966 652380
Settle Market P ☎ 01729 825192
Skipton High St ☎ 01756 792809

Geographers name this sort of landscape after the Karst region of old Yugoslavia, and Craven is absolutely classic Karst scenery. The hills are not so rugged as to be inaccessible to four wheels, and small roads criss-cross the area, calling in on **Malham** from where it's a stroll to the huge cliff of **Malham Cove**, an extraordinary limestone pavement, and the gorge and waterfall in **Gordale Scar**. **Malham Tarn** is the source of the River Aire which, after a spell underground, winds southwards to **Gargrave** where it picks up the Leeds and Liverpool Canal as a travelling partner for the remaining five miles to **Skipton**. A market town of fair size, Skipton is unquestionably the capital of the Craven district and one that, although not in the national park, proudly labels itself 'Gateway to the Dales'.

1 SETTLE & AROUND

Settle grew as a small market town at the crossing of two important trade routes. It still has its market but passing trade is much less now since the A65 bypassed the town. Settle really would have been a sleepy backwater if its other transport link had deserted it, as it very nearly did in the 1980s, but the **Settle–Carlisle railway line** remains open, and attracts many of the town's visitors. Settle itself is unassuming with nothing really exceptional to crow about but I like it for all that, especially the maze of old streets creeping up the hillside towards Upper Settle and Castlebergh, the wooded crag that peers over everything.

"Settle itself is unassuming with nothing really exceptional to crow about but I like it for all that."

A short stroll over the river via a small footbridge will bring you to the photogenic village of **Giggleswick** with two notable places of worship, a private boarding school chapel with a striking copper dome and the parish church with a very unusual name. Only two St Alkelda's churches are to be found in the country – this one and one at

Middleham in Wensleydale where she lived, died and was sainted. If her name is obscure, what about the manner of her death; not many nuns meet their end by being strangled to death by two Viking women using a napkin!

Settle's biggest attribute is the river and fell scenery around it and one six-mile loop walk gives a taste of both. The outward leg, upstream on the Giggleswick bank, is actually on the route of the Ribble Way which takes in the hamlet of Stackhouse on the way to **Stainforth**. Here is an old pack horse bridge to cross and the impressive waterfall of **Stainforth Force** to admire; keep an eye open for leaping salmon in late autumn. For half-way refreshment, try the pub in Stainforth. On leaving the Craven Heifer, the footpath back first scales **Stainforth Scar** before contouring the hillside along to Settle via Langcliffe, giving a bird's-eye view of your outward journey all the way.

¶ FOOD & DRINK

For such a small town Settle is rich in good places to eat. The pick of the restaurants for me are: **Ravenous** (Market Pl ✆ 01729 822277 – excellent restaurant specialising in themed evenings), **Ruchee** (Commercial Courtyard ✆ 01729 823393 – a warm welcome and delicious Indian cuisine), **The Fisherman** (Church St ✆ 01729 823927 – top-quality fish and chips to eat in or take-away), and **Thirteen** (Duke St ✆ 01729 824356 – officially a café/bar, but also offers beers and particularly good steaks).

For a brew and a snack, the best two cafés are **Ye Olde Naked Man** (Market Pl ✆ 01729 823230); and **Poppies** (Bishopdale Court ✆ 07932 182293 ⏱ www.poppiestearoom. blogspot.co.uk). My cycling friends particularly rate the cheap and cheerful **Settle Down** Duke St ✆ 01729 822480.

Pubs

The best pub options are across the river into Giggleswick, with one pub for eating and one for drinking:

Craven Arms Brackenber Lane, Giggleswick BD24 OEB ✆ 01729 825627 ⏱ www.craven-arms-giggleswick.co.uk. Exceptional food with meat from the landlord's own organic farm up the road. 'Looked after properly from pasture to plate,' is their watchword. Occasional cookery demonstrations. B&B available.

Harts Head Inn Belle Hill, Giggleswick BD24 OBA ✆ 01729 82086 ⏱ www. hartsheadhotel.co.uk. Not the most attractive building, but the best beer drinker's pub in the vicinity by a country mile. An ever-changing range of real ales; always a choice of at least four including local brews. Food is reasonably priced, and there's a fair range. B&B available.

2 THE SETTLE–CARLISLE LINE

 www.settle-carlisle.co.uk.

Some who have heard of this famous line assume that it is one of those privately run steam railways re-opened and kept going by volunteers at weekends. In fact it is part of the National Rail network, with a regular scheduled service. The line never did quite close but it came to within a hair's breadth of it in the 1980s and its present fame owes more than a little to the vociferous and successful campaign for its salvation. The Settle–Carlisle line was, and is, so well loved because of its spectacularly scenic qualities and – it has to be said from an engineering point of view – daft route.

In the 1860s, the Midland Railway Company relied on goodwill from the owners of the two existing lines to Scotland, the London and North Eastern Railway and the London and North Western Railway, to transport its freight and passengers north. When the companies fell out, the Midland had no alternative but to build its own line along the only route left available; not the flat land to the east or west of the Pennines, but straight up the middle and over them. This resulted in an incredible 72 miles of line possessing 14 tunnels and 20 viaducts; arguably the most stunning route in the country, providing an ever-changing catalogue of panoramas. Scarcely a moment passes when you are not crossing a towering viaduct over a hillside beck or emerging from the darkness of a tunnel to be presented with another valley and another vista. Marvellous!

"The Settle–Carlisle line is so well loved because of its spectacularly scenic qualities and daft route."

Although the line is busier now than ever in its history, those 1980s campaigners and their 21st-century counterparts are not complacent. Various interested charities and trusts have teamed up to form the Settle–Carlisle partnership and their joint website is the definitive reference point for anything to do with this iconic railway line. For the most spectacular section, ride from Settle as far as Appleby-in-Westmorland.

3 SKIPTON

In Yorkshire Dales terms this is a large town. It owes its origins to those white, woolly, grass-eaters in the surrounding fields – hence the 'sheep-town' label. Its commercial and industrial prominence owes more to its rail and canal links with the bigger towns of West Yorkshire.

All the wool and cotton mills are closed now, but the railways are always busy, taking commuters out to Keighley, Bradford and Leeds, and bringing tourists in. Many of these visitors do use Skipton as a gateway to the rest of the Dales, but lots don't get any further, as there are a wealth of diversions to occupy them in and around the town. The **Leeds and Liverpool Canal** is a big draw, whether you're chugging along it on a narrowboat, strolling beside it on the towpath or just sitting in a waterside café or pub watching other people chug or stroll. I think that the most attractive bit of the canal is a small dead end offshoot called the Spring Branch that curls around the back of **Skipton Castle** giving walking access to Skipton Woods – well worth a potter, especially in May when the carpets of wild garlic and bluebells beneath the trees are at their peak.

If you fancy more than a short potter along the canal towpath the walks up the main canal in either direction are pleasant enough. The western route, ten miles there and back to Gargrave, has an alternative return on footpaths following the railway line. Eastwards takes you to **Low Bradley**, which together with neighbouring **High Bradley** shares a school with the quaint joint name of Bradleys Both. A return riverside footpath completes a six-mile circuit, which can be extended slightly to visit the village of **Cononley**, if only for half-way refreshment in its cracking little pub.

Skipton Castle

☎ 01756 792442 🖱 www.skiptoncastle.co.uk.

I'm a bit fussy about castles. All too often I find them, and abbeys for that matter, a little samey; a set of ruins given the standard English Heritage treatment, but Skipton Castle is definitely not in that category.

What makes it different is its completeness; it is a fully roofed and incredibly well preserved medieval building, a fact for which we have one woman to thank – Lady Anne Clifford. She was the incumbent owner at the time of the Civil War when Skipton Castle, a Royalist stronghold, held out under siege for three years before finally falling to Parliamentarian forces in 1645.

"I'm a bit fussy about castles. All too often I find them a little samey, but Skipton Castle is definitely not in that category."

On Oliver Cromwell's personal instructions the castle was 'Puld downe and demolisht allmost to the foundacon', and that could have been it – another ruin. However, in 1658, with the monarchy restored, and that bounder Cromwell gone, Lady Anne set-to rebuilding the castle, finally, personally planting a yew tree in the central courtyard to celebrate the completion in 1659. Ironically, Lady Anne was the last Clifford to live in Skipton Castle as she died without heir and the estate was sold.

I am a little embarrassed at how many trips to Skipton it took me to finally visit the castle. I suspect many visitors like me admire the magnificent gatehouse but, because the main building is only two storeys high and all hidden behind trees, assume that there's not much else to see, but there is, with over 20 rooms to visit (and children's activities too). Check for special events because these can really make your visit memorable; I was lucky enough to be there in May during the War of the Roses re-enactment, which the children watching got really excited about, and so did I, if I'm honest. The boy next to me said, 'I liked the sword fight best when they were really going at it and clanging their swords. It's a good job they were wearing armour 'cos they could easily have chopped each other's arms off. I wish I could have had a go with my brother.'

"It's a good job they were wearing armour 'cos they could easily have chopped each other's arms off. I wish I could have had a go with my brother."

⚑ FOOD & DRINK

J Stanforth – Celebrated Pork Pie Establishment Mill Bridge ✆ 01756 793477. Their pork pies are so delicious that customers write poetry about them: 'When in Skipton, call and get one/Stanforth's are the best/If you walk by and get no pie/You'll curse the day you left.' They also sell other locally sourced meat products.

The Narrowboat Victoria St ✆ 01756 797992 🖰 www.markettowntaverns.co.uk. A refreshing change this, a wine bar that has reverted to a pub, and a good one at that. A wide range of North Country and European beers always includes Black Sheep and Timothy Taylors, the wine list is reasonable and the food all fresh and home-cooked. Despite its size, the building has an intimate feel, particularly the upstairs gallery area which sports a unique canal mural.

Russian Tea Room High St ✆ 01756 795939 🖰 www.russiantearoom.co.uk. Take your pick of 150 tea varieties, to drink in or take home. Also traditional Russian cuisine as a snack or in the restaurant.

Tempest Arms Elslack BD23 3AY ✆ 01282 842450 🖰 www.tempestarms.co.uk. A 16th-century inn regarded equally highly by connoisseurs of food, beer, wine and comfort. The atmosphere is friendly and relaxed and the food traditional English, all sourced locally. House beer is Moorhouses and guests include Dark Horse's Hetton Pale Ale.

Verdes Swadford St ✆ 01756 700822 🖱 www.verdes.biz. A multi-purpose establishment. Delicatessen and coffee shop open every day and a restaurant (Fri and Sat evenings) with a very good local reputation.

4 EMBSAY & BOLTON ABBEY STEAM RAILWAY

Oh Dr Beeching, what have you done? Only five miles of the original Skipton–Ilkley railway remain and three of those are managed by the volunteers of the Yorkshire Dales Railway Museum Trust. They operate trains, mainly steam, between Embsay and Bolton Abbey, every Sunday of the year and every day in August (✆ 01756 710614 🖱 www.embsayboltonabbeyrailway.org.uk). While this is a fun 15-minute nostalgic experience it is not a particularly useful mode of transport from A to B. Now, if the steam railway succeed in their negotiations with Network Rail to access the remaining two miles of line and Skipton Station, that would be a different matter. I would be tempted to take myself and my bike (free) from Skipton to Bolton Abbey and start my cycling there. Both stations have a shop and café, and you may be tempted by occasional special events like Thomas the Tank Engine day for the little ones, or Strawberry and Cream evening specials and first-class Stately Specials for the big ones.

5 GARGRAVE

The name Gargrave is old English for triangular wood but the trees that led to this label are long gone, cleared to make way for the host of transport links that squeeze through this narrow section of Airedale. The Leeds and Liverpool Canal and Skipton–Lancaster railway have both had their golden age, but the A65 trunk road through the village has never been busier. Pennine Way walkers have to dodge the traffic as they cross on their way north and the villagers are understandably campaigning for a bypass.

Gargrave has one or two points of interest to occupy visitors, notably the site of a Roman Villa, a neat arched stone bridge over the river and canalside walks, but to be honest most travellers pass through.

🍴 FOOD & DRINK

The Dalesman Café High St, Gargrave BD23 3LX ✆ 01756 749250. Particularly popular among cyclists. Wear Lycra if you don't want to feel out of place. No-nonsense and good-value food and drink in a tea shop doubling as a traditional sweet shop.

6 HETTON, RYLSTONE & CRACOE

Some visitors head on a minor road north, a welcome respite from the A65, and find themselves in **Hetton**, a sleepy hamlet with an exceptional pub, the Angel Inn, and a farm-based brewer. The Dark Horse Brewery is one of the newest and smallest breweries in the Dales but is fast earning itself a formidable reputation for quality. 'We're just concentrating on keeping the beer consistent and growing the business slowly,' said brewer Richard Eyton-Jones. 'So the fact that our Hetton Pale Ale managed to win a "Yorkshire's perfect pint" trophy recently was a bonus.'

"The Dark Horse Brewery is one of the smallest in the Dales but is fast earning a formidable reputation for quality."

Nearby, **Rylstone** is a humble hamlet that no-one would have heard of had it not been for the exploits of its Women's Institute. It was they that famously took their clothes off for a calendar photo shoot to raise money for leukaemia research, a story told in the film *Calendar Girls*. Many of the photos were taken down the road in the Devonshire Arms, the village pub of **Cracoe**. Look out for the village postman – he was one of the few people to appear in the film as himself.

A choice of two enchanting walks links these three villages, a two-mile low- level potter along Chapel Lane or a five-mile circuit including the war memorial on the summit of Cracoe Fell.

¶¶ FOOD & DRINK

The Angel Inn Hetton BD23 6LT ☎ 01756 730263 ⌂ www.angelhetton.co.uk. An old drovers' inn with a good balance – staunchly traditional with well-kept local ales, including the village's own brew, but also a stylish and fashionable eatery. The menu is seasonal and has a European slant with an excellent selection of wines to accompany. Very popular, booking advised.

Jacksons of Cracoe Cracoe BD23 6LB ☎ 01756 730269 ⌂ www.jacksonsofcracoe.co.uk. This is basically a butchers with a twist. Not only can you buy top-quality local meat, including limestone beef, but also they have some of the best sausages in Yorkshire, homemade cakes and preserves and Brymoor Farm ice cream (see page 132). The in-house tea shop allows you to sit in and sample the local produce.

7 MALHAM & AROUND

⌂ **Airton Meeting House** Airton (see page 174)

The first time that I visited Malham I was astonished at how small it was. How could such an insignificant hamlet be so well known? The truth is that it's not the buildings of Malham itself that are famous but the surrounding countryside; **Malham Cove**, **Gordale Scar** and **Malham Tarn** primarily. Hundreds of thousands of people come to see these natural wonders and they need somewhere to stay, park, eat and drink, so a service machine has developed including two pubs, three cafés, 11 places to stay and the National Park Centre to tell you about it all. Ironically, some visitors don't make it any further than the village; they see a picture of Gordale Scar in the visitor centre, buy a postcard of the cove, have a cup of tea and drive to the next place without seeing anything real – which is such a shame because the real things here are magnificent. Malham has two big events during the year, an animal-themed activity week called the **Malham Safari** during Whit week and the much more traditional **Malham Show** on August Bank Holiday Saturday.

Upper Airedale has two other villages, **Kirkby Malham** a mile downstream from Malham, and **Airton** the same distance again. Both are peaceful modest places with unusual buildings used as hostels. Kirkby Malham's is the Parish Hall (✆ 01729 830277) and Airton's the Friends' Meeting House (✆ 01729 830263; see page 174 for listing). Kirkby also has the parish church for the whole dale, a 15th-century building on a much older site, and the best pub in the dale, the Victoria Hotel. Airton boasts a farm shop selling all sorts of local produce, and cups of tea, at Town End Farm (✆ 01729 830902).

Malham Cove

I am not sure which experience of Malham Cove has left the biggest impression on me: the first time I stood below it gazing at the breathtaking scale of the curved wall in front maybe, or later that same day lying at the top with just my face over the overhang lip and 260 feet of dizzying space below. Wherever it is viewed from, this is an awe-inspiring place that well deserves its ranking in a recent list of Seven Natural Wonders of Britain.

"Wherever it is viewed from, this is an awe-inspiring place that well deserves its ranking in a list of Seven Natural Wonders of Britain."

The geology of the area seems simple; a beck flows out of Malham Tarn just over a mile north of the cove, but very quickly disappears underground as limestone rivers often do. The dry valley continues southwards, finishing as a notch at the top of the cove, and a river appears from the foot of the cliff. The obvious assumption is that it is the same water top and bottom and the river used to flow over the top of the cliff, creating the cove by erosion –

"You really need to get close up to Malham Cove to experience the full effect."

but not so. The reality is a lot more deceptive: the cliff was formed millions of years ago by an upthrust of the mid-Craven fault. Much later, at the end of the last ice age, meltwater from a glacier formed a monstrous waterfall that eroded the cove four miles back into the hillside and sculpted it into its present curving shape. When the ice melted, the waterfall disappeared. Just to make it even more confusing, water-dye experiments have shown that the water from Malham Tarn does not reappear at the cove but travels at a lower level, reaching the surface south of the village at Aire Head Spring. The beck that bubbles out at the base of the cove is a different river entirely.

You really need to get close up to Malham Cove to experience the full effect; fortunately it is easily accessible for everyone, wheelchair users included. An easy mile from the main car park/bus stop brings you to the bottom of the cove from where you can marvel at the scenery, admire climbers scaling the crag or visit the RSPB base and watch the nesting peregrine falcons. Other birds to look out for here are little owls, green woodpeckers and one of the few natural-site nesting colonies of house-martins. The steep slog up the Pennine Way to the top of the cove is worth the effort because the **limestone pavement** behind the cliff edge is a lush arctic/alpine rock garden in summer. Rarities like alpine bartsia, mountain pansy, bird's-eye primrose and mountain avens all thrive here in the sheltered crevices, or grykes.

Gordale Scar

When the 19th-century romantic artists and writers went in search of wild nature in Britain some of them discovered Gordale Scar and were suitably impressed. Wordsworth attempted to persuade others to visit: 'Let thy feet repair to Gordale-chasm, terrific as the lair where the young lions crouch.' Not modern-day brochure-speak, but he obviously liked it here. Thomas Gray the poet was a little more delicate; he declared that he could only bear to stay for quarter of an hour, and even then 'not without shuddering'. All agreed that no painting could do justice to the scale of the ravine, except James Ward who solved the problem by producing one of the largest canvases ever attempted. His 14-foot by 12-foot painting is regarded as one of the most important 'sublime landscapes' of its time, and hangs in Tate Britain.

So, does it merit all the hype? Yes, is the answer. Gordale Scar is impressive enough as a deep and fairly dry canyon now, but it must have been a terrifying place when the glacial meltwater river that excavated it was still raging. Despite its drama, Gordale is remarkably accessible along its flat lower section, about a third of a mile of wheelchair-negotiable track to the foot of the dual waterfall. It's even more convenient for those staying at Gordale Campsite (℡ 01729 830333) as this will save you the walk from Malham (there is no parking at Gordale). If you do arrive on foot, a convenient alternative return route to Malham is to follow Gordale Beck downstream as it leaps over Janet's Foss, and babbles through Wedber Wood *en route* to join the newly emerged River Aire. It is possible to escape out of the top end of Gordale Scar, but it does require a serious scramble alongside the waterfalls. It is worth doing, just for the fun of it, but it will also lead you towards Malham Tarn and make a fantastic full-day, eight-mile walk possible, linking all of Malham's celebrity venues – the cove, the foss, the scar and the tarn.

> *"Gordale Scar is impressive enough now, but it must have been a terrifying place when the glacial meltwater river that excavated it was still raging."*

Malham Tarn

The Malham Tarn estate is now under the stewardship of the National Trust but a clue to one of its earliest owners lies in the name of the highest fell in the region. At 2,169 feet above sea level, Fountains Fell rises over nearly 12 square miles of prime limestone sheep country, and reminds us of the huge power and influence the monks of Fountains Abbey had, from a good 25 miles away near Ripon. After the dissolution of the monasteries the estate passed through many hands and finished up in the possession of the Morrison family. In the 1850s James Morrison converted what was a Georgian hunting lodge into Tarn House, then promptly died, leaving the estate and an awful lot of money to his son Walter. As a very rich socialite, Walter invited all and sundry up to Malham with celebrity guests including influential thinkers John Ruskin, Charles Darwin and John Stuart Mill. Writer Charles Kingsley was a regular visitor and much of his *Water Babies* was inspired by Malham Tarn.

In 1946 the last private owner of the estate bequeathed it to the National Trust and with them it remains, although they do lease Tarn House itself to the **Field Studies Council** (FSC ✆ 01729 830331 🖱 www.field-studies-council.org/centres/malhamtarn) as a residential centre for the study of environmental sciences. The FSC run over 30 different courses a year on subjects as diverse as earthworms and other invertebrates, painting the flora of Malham Tarn, and the geology of the Dales. Their choice of venue is a good one because the tarn itself is a **National Nature Reserve**, ecologically important through being one of only eight upland alkaline lakes in Europe. The lake has breeding great crested and little grebes with winter bringing more waterfowl like pochard, wigeon, teal and goosanders. Alongside the open water are rich floral fen and bog areas. Access to all of the nature reserve is free of charge except for a wheelchair-accessible boardwalk across the bog which has a token entrance fee. The National Trust also produce very informative leaflets for four **waymarked walks** around the estate, from an easy 4½ miles around the tarn to an eight-mile yomp up Fountains Fell. Another excellent leaflet is for a 4½-mile family **bike ride**. All can be obtained from their visitor centre in Malham village or are downloadable from their website (🖱 www.nationaltrust.org.uk).

🍴 FOOD & DRINK

Old Barn Café Malham BD23 4DA ✆ 01729 830486. A nice, small unfussy café (muddy boots welcome) in the village centre. All-day breakfast recommended.

Town End Farm Tea Room Scosthrop, Airton BD23 4BE ✆ 01729 830902. Part of a farm shop on a working farm, and selling snacks and drinks. Closed Mon.

Victoria Hotel Kirkby Malham BD23 4BS ✆ 01729 830499. A quiet and peaceful village pub and, because of that, easily my favourite in the dale. Changing list of mainly Yorkshire cask ales.

MID WHARFEDALE

Most of the River Wharfe's length is downstream of the Yorkshire Dales, and into the county of West Yorkshire, but our interest lies upstream in its mid-section. **Bolton Abbey** sits at the border, just in North Yorkshire and the national park, and Mid Wharfedale continues nearly ten miles northwards from here to the small town of **Grassington**, with much to please in between.

8 BOLTON ABBEY

🏠 **Barden Bunkbarn**, Barden and **Beamsley Hospital Almshouse**, Beamsley (see page 174)

The ecclesiastical remains at the tiny village of Bolton so dominate, that the whole place is now called Bolton Abbey. Ironically, for a building that was never completed, it is one of the most intact priories in the country with the original nave still used as the **priory church of St Mary and St Cuthbert**. Location, location, location – that must have been the watchword for 12th-century monks. This riverside site ranks with Rievaulx and Fountains as one of the most awe-inspiring positions for an abbey anywhere. No wonder the Augustinians moved here from their original priory in Embsay. At the Dissolution, all the Abbey lands were given to the Duke of Devonshire and the Cavendish family still own and operate the estate (🖰 www.boltonabbey.com).

Their lands extend upstream to include **Strid Wood** and **Barden Tower** and on the other side of the river, the wide tracts of **Barden Moor**. These are the places to head for if you are seeking solitude because most visitors stay around the priory or on the riverbanks between Bolton Bridge and a charismatic Victorian building, the **Cavendish Pavilion**. This is still doing what it was designed for in 1898, serving tea and cakes to thousands of visitors from the industrial cities of West Yorkshire, although the menu and catchment area are both a lot more extensive now. Children won't be interested in that though; once they have had their ice cream they will be drawn like magnets to the river to paddle, fish for minnows and swim in the deeper pools, and it is safe to do so

A walk from Bolton Abbey

✳ OS Explorer map OL2; start: Bolton Abbey, grid reference SE075541.

My favourite walk from Bolton Abbey is a longer one that includes Strid Woods but continues up river following the route of the Dales Way to Howgill. Here a permissive path climbs through the woods to open fell-side and ultimately the summit of Simon's seat. The return journey takes in Barden Fell and descends the spectacular Valley of Desolation, again on a permissive path. At the end of this 8½-mile walk, if your legs are up to it, detour a couple of hundred yards up the road to Laund House to pay your respects to a venerable old-timer. The Laund Oak, by the roadside, is one of the oldest oak trees in the country, a peer of the Sherwood Forest Major Oak, and over 800 years old.

here unless the river is running high and fast. The estate doesn't actively encourage swimming but they don't discourage it either, which is good. Rod fishing is also possible in the river; trout or grayling day tickets can be purchased, and it's obviously best where the swimmers and paddlers aren't. Tuition is also available.

If you have children who are not interested in the river, or it is too cold or flooded, there are other things to keep them interested; a Green Man trail or nature bingo in Strid Wood or a simple treasure hunt on the welcome leaflet. For really enquiring youngsters or mature learners, the estate produces two teachers' packs with worksheets that are just as interesting for adults and families. The *Valley of Desolation* pack improved my walk up Barden Moor no end – I learnt loads about the geology, natural history and the past flood damage that gave the place its name.

"The estate doesn't actively encourage swimming but they don't discourage it either."

Sample local **arts and crafts** at Strid Wood Exhibition Centre where ceramics, paintings and furniture are on display. You may even see Richard Law, the bodger, at work if you are in Strid Wood as he has his outdoor workshop there (www.flyingshavings.co.uk). If you fancy actually doing the art yourself then drawing and painting classes are available from professional artist Nigel Overton, at the Tea Cottage, most summer Saturdays (01943 608447 www.overtonfinearts.co.uk).

The estate also runs almost monthly **Country Fairs** throughout the year in the main car park, a great mixture of farmers' market and art and craft display. Other **events** worth finding out about if they float your boat are kite workshops (Fridays in the summer holidays), giant puppet shows, autumn fungus walks and Christmas carol singing.

Strid Wood

This area of woodland, though not very big or containing any especially rare or spectacular species, is a delight. The trees, mainly oak, cling to the deep sides of Strid Gorge and support a rich population of birds in the spring and fungi in the autumn. The dawn chorus here in June features all the signature woodland birds of Yorkshire: redstarts, pied and spotted flycatchers and wood warblers. Dead wood is drummed on and excavated into by green and great spotted woodpeckers, and nuthatches and treecreepers scuttle around on the wrinkled trunks.

The woods are special, but it is the River Wharfe that makes this place exceptional, and gives it the name.

Strid is local dialect for stride and refers to one place where the river narrows to a step's width across. In reality it is more like a leap, and a brave one at that, because the whole river thunders through the gap below. The Strid is even more dangerous than it seems because both banks are actually suspended ledges of limestone covering deep undercuts on both sides. Numerous swimmers over the years have been taken under them by wayward currents and drowned. On less vigorous stretches of the river dippers bob on the rocks, grey wagtails leap for flies in sunny spots and, if you're lucky, a common sandpiper will trill its alarm as it disappears upstream.

"The trees cling to the deep sides of Strid Gorge and support a rich population of birds in the spring and fungi in the autumn."

Six waymarked trails can be found in Strid Wood, some very short and wheelchair accessible and all less than two miles long. They can get very crowded on summer weekends, especially on the car park side of the river.

Barden Tower

This imposing building has lots going for it, not least the fact that wandering around it is completely free of charge. Despite its name, it is more than just a tower, but not quite a castle, and has had a few changes of role in its long life. Originally a Norman hunting lodge, it was later extended into a fortified house by Sir Henry Clifford, who fancied living in the country rather than Skipton Castle. That accomplished renovator, Lady Anne Clifford, got her two-penny-worth in during the 1650s but on her death the tower passed to the Earls of Cork and fell into decline. After a spell as a farmhouse in the late 18th century it was abandoned.

The building next door to the tower was never abandoned: the Priest's House was built by Sir Henry Clifford for his personal chaplain and is now what must be one of the most atmospheric restaurants in the country. The old stables of the tower next door have been converted into a very convenient self-catering bunkhouse for large parties of evening diners in the restaurant – or anyone else wanting accommodation in this desirable spot. If you fill it with 24 people it costs less than £8 per person per night. See *Accommodation*, page 174.

🍴 FOOD & DRINK

The Cavendish Pavilion BD23 6EX 📞 01756 710245 🖱 www.cavendishpavilion.co.uk.
There are five cafés in Bolton Abbey, the pick of them on location alone is this, and you can
sit outside. Food is good but a bit pricey, although the afternoon tea special is good value.
The Priest's House Restaurant Barden Towers, Barden BD23 6AS 📞 01756 720616
🖱 www.thepriestshouse.co.uk. A unique Grade 1 listed building and really good-quality
food. Not a huge menu but all done well. Sunday lunch is particularly good value and in
good weather when the tea terrace operates as a café, there can't be many more pleasant
places to be. Very popular so book early. Open Thu–Sun lunch and Fri and Sat evenings.

Pubs

Pubs are in short supply in Bolton Abbey but three miles down the road (and into West
Yorkshire) Addingham has two worth calling in on:
The Fleece Main St, Addingham 📞 01943 830491 🖱 www.thefleeceaddingham.co.uk.
Excellent food, passable beer.
The Swan Main St, Addingham 📞 01943 831999 🖱 www.swan-addingham.co.uk.
Excellent beer, passable food.

9 GRASSINGTON

'Now that's a good question and I wish you had asked someone else,'
said the welcoming lady at the Devonshire Institute reception. 'I could
flannel on for ten minutes trying to answer it but, to be honest, I don't
know. If you do find out come back and tell me.'

My question was a simple one, or so I thought. 'Is Grassington a
town or a village?' I had been given a variety of conflicting answers
by other locals up to this point. 'Village of course … too small for
a town' (barmaid). 'Town I think. Isn't that what the "ton" means?'
(local artist). 'No, this is a village, Skipton's the town' (farmer). The
definitive answer is that it is a town; the official reason being it
was granted a charter for a market and fair in 1282. Grassington
has played a few roles in its time, originally as the name suggests
as a place for grazing cattle, then a market for selling them. The
town was very involved with both the long-gone lead mining and
textile booms, and the railway made a fleeting visit then left again.
Now this is the administrative centre for Upper Wharfedale in the
background but its public face, especially from Easter to October, is
tourism. Grassington is one of the best loved and most visited places
in the Dales. It has a National Park Centre, small folk museum, three

pubs, five cafés and numerous art and craft shops, mostly clustered around the Market Square.

The creative theme reaches its peak during two weeks in late June every year when the town is completely taken over by a **music and arts festival** (⌁ www.grassington-festival.org) – a wonderful mix of everything from big-name comedians to school brass bands, magician or dry-stone walling workshops, jazz, opera, folk, rock and world music, readings, plays, and visual arts displays in houses and fields … you name it and it's here. It doesn't all stop in winter either; three Saturdays in December, in the run-up to Christmas, the town goes all Victorian with a Dickensian festival.

If the crowds in town get too much, two nearby rural diversions are within easy walking distance, **Grass Wood** upstream and **Linton Falls** in the opposite direction. If you continue downstream on the Dales Way footpath, or back roads, there are a series of very photogenic and individual villages to visit: **Burnsall** right on the river and **Hebden** and **Appletreewick** just above it.

Grass Wood

As I'm a naturalist, this is one of my favourite places in the Dales – no, not just in the Dales, anywhere. A circular walk from Grassington of not much more than three miles takes in one of the most beautiful stretches of the River Wharfe, a Woodland Trust Reserve, a Yorkshire Wildlife Trust Nature Reserve and one of the most important archaeological sites in Yorkshire. Doing the route clockwise the river comes first and, if it is warm enough, you may be tempted to have a swim in one of the deep pools. The Wharfe is probably the best river in Yorkshire for wild swimming (see page 10) and this mile section is one of its best but take care near Ghaistrill's Strid; it is another powerful 'narrows' with dangerous undercuts like its Bolton Abbey namesake.

"If you are lucky enough to be here in early summer, the floral display once you enter the wood will blow you away if you are that way inclined."

If you are lucky enough to be here in early summer, the floral display once you enter the wood will blow you away if you are that way inclined. This is an ancient woodland designated as a Site of Special Scientific Interest and especially rich in flower species; carpets of bluebells in May give way to betony, St John's wort, basil, marjoram, lily of the valley and herb paris to name but a few. Keep an eye out for orchids as some rare ones have a foothold here.

Higher up on the hillside as the trees thin to meadow on the limestone pavement, butterflies are everywhere: fritillaries, peacocks, blues and heaths, and the rare northern brown argus if you are lucky. Another scarce insect lives here – the yellow ant; you may well not see them but the distinctive grassy humps of their anthills testify to the antiquity of the meadows.

"For 2,000 years the inhabitants of the Dales have been gradually moving their homes down towards the river, leaving faint footprints behind – Bronze Age at the top, Iron Age and medieval in sequence lower down."

The return route to Grassington is on the Dales Way footpath passing extensive archaeological remains of old settlements. For 2,000 years the inhabitants of the Dales have been gradually moving their homes down towards the river, leaving faint footprints behind – Bronze Age at the top, Iron Age and medieval in sequence lower down.

Linton & Linton Falls

The dramatic natural cataract of Linton Falls on the River Wharfe is nearer to Grassington than the village of Linton, so the choice of name is a little odd. It possibly has something to do with the church on the riverbank a quarter of a mile downstream. This is Linton's parish **church of St Michael and All Angels**, a long name for a tiny medieval building but in a magical setting. The church is even further from the village than the falls, probably because it re-uses the site of an earlier pagan shrine, so it is perhaps apt that the Green Man, a pagan symbol, should be carved into the church roof timbers. Despite there being no footpath from the river to Linton village it is still worth strolling up the road for half a mile to see the pretty village green and packhorse bridge and have a meal or drink in the Fountaine Inn. If water levels are low enough you can re-cross the river via stepping stones to return to Grassington.

⫶ FOOD & DRINK

Grassington has lots of cafés close together, a sign of healthy competition and good quality all round.

THE FITTON FAMILY FLAG

Burnsall Feast Sports are rife with tradition, none more closely followed than the fixing of the flag on race day. This job has fallen to the Fitton family since the 1930s, as Chris Fitton recalls.

'I don't know how old I was when I first climbed the fell on Sports Day, possibly four or five. My father had been doing it for many years prior to the war and established it as a family ritual. The object of the exercise was to carry the flag up and put it securely into the cairn which still stands proud at the top of Burnsall Fell. Then, as now, it represented blessed relief to aching legs as the halfway point that all competitors in the Classic Fell Race must pass prior to the heart-stopping descent.

Since that first time around 1948, I and assorted family members have climbed the fell faithfully every year. The group of between five and ten has included pregnant mothers, newly born toddlers, grandchildren, children, adults up to their late seventies together with boyfriends, girlfriends and occasionally somewhat reluctant strangers who, full of ale in the Red Lion the night before, having heard of the annual pilgrimage swore they would join us and more often than not, did. This motley group would always assemble around 07.00 outside the car park hopefully with the flag. The flag is, and always was, the great problem. No-one can ever find it.

Committee members provide storage space for the various accoutrements of the Sports Day, and the night before it is all brought down to the green. As often as not, the flag is missing. Over the years it has taken the shape of an old cream bed sheet, a St George's flag, and once, bizarrely, a National Benzole flag.

Sometimes there is a pole but no flag, and sometimes a flag but no pole.

The route taken never varies, and we have a breather at the top of the field before reaching the summit around 7.30, to drain a celebratory flask of whisky once the flag is securely installed. Finally, the view is admired and we stick out our chests and say to each other that we should do this more regularly. We never do.

On our return home, a vast and well-earned breakfast is consumed and I offer up a prayer that whoever brings down that flag gives it to someone who can remember, 12 months later, what he did with it.'

Forester's Arms Main St ✆ 01756 752349 🖰 www.forestersarmsgrassington.co.uk. My favourite pub in Grassington, this is a friendly and welcoming place with well-kept cask Yorkshire beers and good food. I enjoyed the tenderest lamb shank that I have ever had here.
Fountaine Inn Linton BD23 5HJ ✆ 01756 752210 🖰 www.fountaineinnatlinton.co.uk. A welcoming pub in a great setting, tucked into a corner of the village green on the beck-side. Named after a local man who made his fortune in London at the time of the Black Death – burying bodies! Besides cask Tetleys and John Smith's bitters on tap there's also Fountaine Pale Ale, brewed for the pub by Cuerden of West Yorkshire.

10 HEBDEN & BURNSALL

Hebden is a solid little village with a decent café and pub and a very obvious lead-mining past. Lots of small miners' cottages line Mill and Back lanes as they creep down the hill to the river. Stepping stones and a footbridge here allow the Dales Way path to cross the Wharfe on its way to Burnsall. This is a dramatic half mile of water course as the river eats into high limestone banks to form the precipitous crags of Loup Scar and Wilfred Scar, popular 'leaping' rocks into the deep river pools. St Wilfred also gives his name to the very old church close by, but undoubtedly the village's most striking landmark is its graceful five-arched stone bridge spanning the river.

"The river eats into high limestone banks to form the precipitous crags of Loup Scar and Wilfred Scar."

Burnsall's most famous event is its annual fell race which was first run in the 1870s making it the oldest of its kind in the world, a fact that the villagers are fiercely proud of. Evidence that sporting events have been part of the Feast of St Wilfred since before Elizabethan times gives it an even more impressive claim of antiquity. St Wilfred's Day is the first Sunday after 12 August, and the Burnsall feast takes place the following week with the races on the Saturday.

The 'Classic' fell race, as it is called, starts from the bridge with competitors aiming for a flagged cairn on Burnsall Fell about 1½ miles away and 1,000 feet above the village. The best runners make the flag in just over ten minutes, which is quick, but nowhere near their suicidal descent speed, as some of them manage the return in less than three minutes.

¶¶ FOOD & DRINK

The Red Lion Burnsall BD23 6BU ✆ 01756 720204 🖰 www.redlion.co.uk. An ancient building with 900-year-old cellars that have a resident ghost who likes to turn the beer pumps off. Food features game in season and locally sourced meats and cheeses. A range of cask beers are served, most from Yorkshire.

Wharfe View Tearooms The Green, Burnsall YO23 6BS ✆ 01756 720237. A basic but welcoming café, very popular with walkers and bikers.

11 APPLETREEWICK

🏠 **Knowles Lodge B&B** (see page 174)

If ever a name conjures up pastoral loveliness it's this one, but over the years locals have tired of the full tongue-twisting mouthful and shortened it to 'Aptrick'. Sunday name or not this is a very agreeable place, especially down in the valley bottom where the river bounces and swirls its way through a series of rapids, beloved of slalom kayakers. Not many villages of this size manage to support a pub these days, but Appletreewick keeps two going comfortably. One of them, the Craven Arms, incorporates the village's most remarkable building, not the pub itself but a cruck barn behind it. This is a new building made to a very old design and with a heather-thatched roof, the first of its kind built for 400 years in the Dales.

I'm sure Aptrick has also produced many remarkable people over the centuries, but for the one that made the biggest impact on the world stage we have to go back to the early 1600s. **William Craven**, a humble village lad, was sent off to London to apprentice as a draper and, to cut a long story short, did quite well for himself. By the time he returned he had made his fortune, earned himself a knighthood, spent a term as Mayor of London and married the king's sister. I can imagine his reception on returning to the snug of the Craven Arms, 'Na then Billy. Tha's not done badly ... tha' round, methinks'.

"I can imagine his reception on returning to the snug of the Craven Arms, 'Na then Billy. Tha's not done badly ... tha' round, methinks.'"

You can take a stroll downstream to the stepping stones near **Howgill**. This is another inviting, swimmable section of river and quiet enough to offer a really good chance of seeing the local wildlife. I know that there are otters and crayfish here, even though I haven't seen either of them alive. On my last swimming visit here I landed on a mid-river rock that held the chewed-up remains of a native white-clawed crayfish, its one remaining claw bearing its furry killer's teeth marks.

FOOD & DRINK

Craven Arms Inn BD23 6DA 01756 720270 www.craven-cruckbarn.co.uk. A wonderfully atmospheric building restored to the original oak beams, flag floor, gas lights and open fires state. Traditional pub games, good food and a range of Yorkshire and Lancashire beers. Open every day.

The New Inn West End BD23 6DA 01756 720252 www.the-new-inn-appletreewick.com. Unspoilt village local, for many years ahead of its time as the only non-smoking pub in the country. Serves a wide range of Yorkshire real ales and good food. Open every day.

12 PARCEVALL HALL GARDENS

BD23 6DE ✆ 01756 720311 ⌂ www.parcevallhallgardens.co.uk.

'Serene' was the word that sprang to mind when I first set foot over the threshold here, which is no surprise, as that is the feeling its creator was trying to achieve. I say 'creator' although Sir William Milner did not build the hall from scratch, but renovated a derelict Elizabethan building in the late 1920s. He definitely did create the garden though, skilfully laying out borders, terraces and woodland – transforming what was previously open agricultural fell-side. Sir William came from a wealthy socialite family, a world that he did not fit in to easily. He was quiet and retiring, writing once of his delight in 'sitting with a friend in front of a roaring log fire, in companionable quiet over coffee'.

"'Serene' was the word that sprang to mind when I first set foot over the threshold here; the feeling its creator was trying to achieve."

He was a deeply religious man so it is apt that his legacy, the hall, is now leased to the church to be used as a retreat, and the rest of us can use the tea room and gardens (✆ 01756 720630) for the same purpose. Slightly at odds with this genteel ambience but testimony to the huge changes Sir William managed here, the hillside above Parcevall Hall is so wild and intimidating, the Anglo-Saxons named one ravine the Troll's Arse, now Trollers Ghyll, and there are still tales of the ghostly dog with giant shining eyes called the Barquest, whose appearance foretold a death.

13 STUMP CROSS CAVERNS

HG3 5JL ✆ 01756 752780 ⌂ www.stumpcrosscaverns.co.uk; closed winter.

The name suggests that there was once an old way-cross near here, on the Grassington to Pateley Bridge packhorse route, but no evidence of it can be found on the ground now. What there are in abundance are tell-tale signs of a lead-mining past: disused levels, tips and literally hundreds of old shafts pock-marking the surface of the moor. It was lead miners searching for more rich seams of metal who discovered the natural fissure at Stump Cross in 1860, but it was worthless to them as a source of ore.

One local man had his finger on the pulse of the burgeoning Victorian tourist industry though, and realised that there was more than one way to make money underground. William Newbould bought the cave and opened it to the public, charging one shilling (5p) per person per visit, a small fortune in those days. In the subsequent 150 years, the Stump Cross cavern system has been extensively explored and found to extend over four miles.

"Most cavers visit just for the thrills, but some important scientific discoveries have also been made along the way."

Most cavers visit just for the thrills, but some important scientific discoveries have also been made along the way. We know, for instance, that the cave was open to the outside about 90,000 years ago, because animal bones dating from this time have been found inside. The Yorkshire Dales must have been a very cold place then, as these remains are from animals that all live in today's Arctic regions. Fragments of skeletons from bison and reindeer have turned up, but the prize find was the well-preserved skull of a wolverine, one of the few ever to be found in Britain. Entry into the cave (with a 20-minute film show) is reasonable value, but if going underground doesn't appeal, then the modern information centre, gift shop and café at ground level are all free of charge to visit.

UPPER WHARFEDALE

🏠 **Cowside** Langstrethdale (see page 174)

Further upstream, Wharfedale heads between the high fells beyond the twin villages of **Kilnsey** and **Conistone**, splitting into the two arms of **Littondale** and **Langstrothdale** which then wrap around the top of Craven in a cosy embrace. Usually, as you head up a hill-country valley, settlements become sparser and smaller; Wharfedale

EXTREME CLIMBING IN WHARFEDALE

At 170 feet high, Kilnsey Crag is not huge, but the glacier that scraped away its bottom section thousands of years ago has left a bizarrely suspended lump of rock that doesn't look as if it should stay up. The 40-foot overhang is a magnet for extreme climbers and there are numerous described routes on Kilnsey Crag. The first person to complete a new route has the honour of naming it; 'Sticky Wicket' I can see the logic of but 'Let them eat Jellybeans'? The most difficult climb, Northern Lights, was climbed in the year 2000 by S McClure and graded 9a – that's 'virtually impossible' to you and me.

does not deviate from this norm, and beyond Grassington there is nothing even remotely resembling a town.

Kettlewell justly claims to be the largest of the Upper Wharfedale villages, and will be familiar if you have seen the film *Calendar Girls*, as this was the location used for much of the action. The valley's only road winds its way through **Starbotton**, and reaches another parting of the ways at **Buckden**. If you are using wheeled transport you have a choice here; right takes you to **Cray** and then over to Bishopdale and Aysgarth and, at 1,400 feet, it is the highest bus route in the Dales – a spectacular run on the number 800 but only once a week in summer (Sunday, noon from Kettlewell returning 16.00 from Hawes). A left turn at Buckden follows the Wharfe through **Hubberholme** and then a much higher pass over the flank of Dodd Fell direct to Hawes – much too high and steep for a bus unfortunately, but an enjoyable drive in a car. If you manage it on a bike, you deserve a medal.

"At 1,400 feet, it is the highest bus route in the Dales – a spectacular run on the number 800 but only once a week in summer."

14 KILNSEY & CONISTONE

These two villages, though they have half a mile of clear valley and a river separating them, have been tied since the 14th century when they were known as Conyston cum Kylnesey. They still have a joint church and village hall (and one of the biggest agricultural shows in the Dales in early September) but Kilnsey has the lion's share of the visitors. This must be partly down to the attention grabbing cliff that looms over the village.

Kilnsey's other big draw is **Kilnsey Park and Trout Farm** (01756 752150 www.kilnseypark.co.uk), a business unashamedly aimed at families with fun fishing, an adventure playground and trails, and cuddly animals to pet. For adults this is a working trout farm where you can learn to fly fish, hire rods, buy smoked, frozen or fresh fish, or just eat it in the restaurant. This is the only place I have ever heard of that does battered trout, chips and peas.

Kilnsey Park is also serious about its environmental impact, generating its own hydro-electric power, and running a red squirrel breeding programme and demonstration beehives in conjunction with Wharfedale Beekeepers Association.

¶¶ FOOD & DRINK

The Tennant's Arms Kilnsey BD23 5PS ☎ 01756 752301 ⌂ www.tennantsarms.co.uk.
A big place with a large central stone-floored bar and smaller opulently decorated rooms.
Slightly unnerving stuffed animals everywhere, but cask Taylors and Black Sheep beer and
very good-value food, especially the Sunday carvery. Open all day weekends.

15 KETTLEWELL

Transport on foot, whether two or four, has long been a theme here.
Kettlewell grew up at the meeting place of packhorse and drovers'
routes and is now quite a centre for walkers, using many of those old
bridleways of course. I'm sure our ancestors would find our walking
for leisure odd though, especially the habit of heading for the highest
hill-tops. Their walks were everyday practical means of journeying from

THE SOLE SURVIVOR

'That plane is too low,' thought 12-year-old Norman Parrington, as he stared up into the snowy sky from his school playground in Kettlewell on 31 January 1942.

The all-Polish, six-man crew of the Wellington bomber that Norman had seen were oblivious to the danger that they were in because of the blizzard, so did not see the summit ridge of Buckden Pike looming up until it was too late. The plane clipped a stone wall at 200mph and hit the mountain, slithering several hundred feet before stopping. The rear gunner's turret, with Joe Fusniak in it, was completely knocked off the aircraft on the initial impact, a fact which probably saved his life.

Concussed, and with a broken ankle, he crawled to the remains of the rest of the plane to find only one companion still alive, and him seriously injured. With the blizzard still raging, Joe realised that he needed to get off the mountain to save both their lives.

He crawled nearly a mile through the snow, hopelessly lost, until he chanced upon a set of fox tracks which eventually led him down to the White Lion Inn at Cray, and safety. Sadly, the Parker family living in the pub couldn't understand Joe's broken English as he tried to explain the plight of his crewmate. By the time he managed to convince them that he wasn't a German pilot, and that a rescue was needed, the weather was too bad to send out a search party. The following day the plane was found, but too late; Joe's friend Jan Sadowski had died in the night.

In 1942 in recognition of his bravery, Sergeant Joseph Fusniak was awarded the British Empire medal by George VI, but was haunted for years afterwards by memories of his lost companions. In 1973 he personally erected a stone cross near the site of the crash, with fragments of the aircraft embedded in its base, and a small sculpture of a fox attached, in thanks to the animal that saved his life.

village to village and valley to valley via the lowest and easiest route. They wouldn't dream of aiming for the summit of **Great Whernside**, which is my favourite destination from Kettlewell. Facilities for modern-day walkers are the **Over and Under** outdoor equipment shop (01756 760871 www.overandunder.co.uk) and a village store.

The ascent of Great Whernside
OS Explorer map OL30; start: Blue Bell Inn, grid reference SD968723.

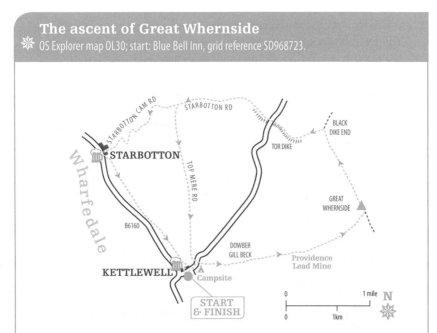

This impressive fell (not to be confused with Whernside) rivals the Three Peaks for altitude but has far fewer visiting walkers. The outward route from Kettlewell tours the full length of the village to Fold Farm campsite then follows Dowber Gill Beck up the hillside, with birds your only company; meadow pipits and wheatears mainly, but ring ouzels breed in the quiet corners. The public footpath stops after a mile or so, at the remains of Providence Lead Mine, but, as this is all open access land, you can head straight up the slope to the summit. You will have earned the next flat mile of ridge walk north, with glorious views of Nidderdale to your right and Wharfedale to the left (weather permitting). After a steep descent to Tor Dike the return route is an historic one along ancient bridleways with an optional mile-and-a-bit extension to Starbotton. Back in Kettlewell you can rehydrate in one of two cafés or three pubs, a fairly good choice but not a patch on the 13 hostelries that existed at the height of the village market's importance a couple of hundred years ago.

⏍ FOOD & DRINK

Zarina's Tea Room Beckside BD23 5QX ✆ 01756 761188 ⌂ www.zarinaskettlewell.co.uk.
If you have a thing about drinking tea from a china cup, you're in luck, and the homemade
cakes are raved about. Also does B&B, where dogs and children go free.

16 BUCKDEN

A Bronze Age stone circle at Yockenthwaite provides archaeological
evidence of people living in this valley for thousands of years, but
Buckden is a relative latecomer. The name gives a clue as to why;
Buck-dene, the valley of deer, refers to the Norman hunting forest
of Langstrothdale and the village was created as their forest keeper's
headquarters. Only later when the forests were cleared and the last
deer had been killed did Buckden become a market town dealing in
sheep and wool. The market is long gone but there is a village store
open every day, a local artists' gallery that doubles as a national park
information point and a farm shop stocked with local Heber Farm
lamb and beef. Like Kettlewell it is now a tourist centre with a high
proportion of visiting walkers.

Most stick to the gentle pastoral strolls in the valley bottom, but
some are tempted up the hill behind the village and **Buckden Pike**
can be a tremendous little excursion. This is not a long walk, less than
two miles from pub to summit, but it is steep and exciting. Normally,
a circular route is just as good done in either direction, but this is
one walk I would always start by following
the direct route up alongside Buckden Beck.
This way the scenic delights are more visible,
a tricky, slippery descent is avoided and my
dodgy knees don't get such a hammering. If
you can manage to be there on a sunny day
after a spell of wet weather then you are in
for a treat because Buckden Beck's descent
is precipitous to say the least. The OS map
mentions three waterfalls, but there are at least four times that number,
of various sizes. High up the hill the beck emerges from the remains
of Buckden lead mine, a peaceful place away from the roar of water to
rest and contemplate. A direct line uphill across open access land will
bring you to the summit ridge; turn left and it's a short stroll to the trig
point at 2,303 feet. Turn right on a short detour and you will arrive at a

*"High up the hill the
beck emerges from the
remains of Buckden
lead mine, a peaceful
place away from the
roar of water to rest
and contemplate."*

cross marked on the map as 'Memorial Cross', the site of dramatic and tragic wartime events (see box, page 179).

There's also a terrific lower-level four-mile circular walk that's potentially a pub crawl – linking up Bucken, Cray and Hubberholme (each of which has a pub). Follow the track rising north from Buckden – you can later drop to Cray and find a path above the pub heading west along a glorious natural terrace, with exquisite views right down Wharfedale. When you reach **Hubberholme**, pop into the church – a beauty, with a rare rood-loft dating back to 1558; from there you can follow the Dales Way back, along the lane and then along the river to Buckden.

¶¶ FOOD & DRINK

The Buck Inn Buckden BD23 5JA ✆ 01756 761401 ⁿ www.thebuckinnbuckden.co.uk. After a period of closure, the Buck has been refurbished and is back in business as the hub of village life. The beer is as good as ever and food is traditional and affordable pub fare. Dog-friendly B&B available.

17 LITTONDALE

This tributary valley of the Wharfe shares with Wensleydale the unusual feature of taking its name from a small village in the dale and not the river. The River Skirfare begins its life at the head of the valley where Foxup Beck and Cosh Beck meet, after which it flows serenely down the middle of a typical small Yorkshire dale past the hamlets of Halton Gill, Litton, Arncliffe and Hawkswick. Remnants of the ancient hunting forest cling to the steep valley sides and support rich mixtures of limestone flowers. Herb paris is one of them and is known as a primary woodland indicator species, one that only grows in very old and undisturbed woodland, so its presence in Hawkswick and Scoska Woods in particular testify to their age.

"Remnants of ancient hunting forest cling to the steep valley sides and support rich mixtures of limestone flowers."

Arncliffe is the largest of the dale's hamlets and takes its name from the days when eagles were found in Yorkshire, 'erne' being the old English name for the white-tailed eagle. Two minor roads link Littondale with neighbouring valleys, Halton Gill to Stainforth in Ribblesdale and Arncliffe to Malham in Airedale. Both routes are spectacular and only

UPDATES WEBSITE

You can post your comments and recommendations, and read the latest feedback and updates from other readers online at www.bradtupdates.com/yorkshiredales.

suitable for healthy cars or very fit and healthy cyclists. It's a shame that they're too steep for buses as they would make superb scenic routes.

¶¶ FOOD & DRINK

The Falcon Inn Arncliffe BD23 5QE ✆ 01756 770205 ⌂ www.thefalconinn.com. A time-warp gem with Timothy Taylors beer straight from the cask in a jug and lunchtime snacks including legendary pie and peas. B&B is on offer and free permits for wild brown trout fishing on the nearby River Skirfare are available to residents.

Queen's Arms Litton BD23 5QJ ✆ 01756 770208. Friendly rustic pub with generous portions of bar food and Litton Ale brewed on the premises.

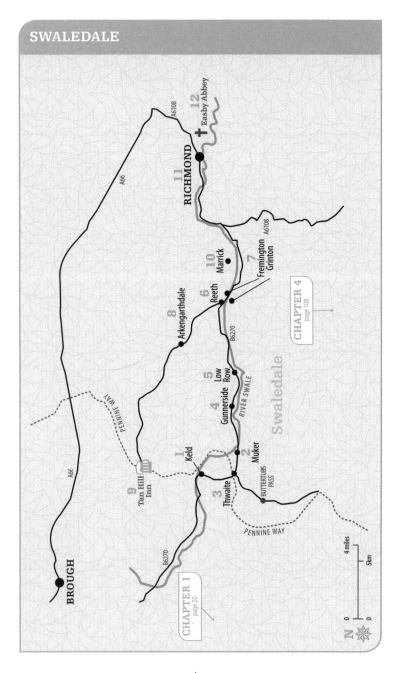

3

SWALEDALE

The Yorkshire Dales vary in character, with each valley possessing its own unique quirks, but Swaledale always seems to me more different than the others. It is a dale apart, with much more of a northern feel to it: place names are almost all unadulterated Norse, woods are few and far between, and people almost as thin on the ground. Swaledale is the least populated of the Dales, with no towns at all above Richmond, and no main roads. It is quiet and wild and for those reasons alone is many people's favourite.

"The Yorkshire Dales vary in character, but Swaledale always seems to me more different than the others. It is a dale apart, woods are few and far between, and people almost as thin on the ground."

For the past thousand years Swaledale's economy and landscape has been shaped by two things, sheep and lead. The lack of trees is down to historical forest clearance for grazing but doesn't come close to the devastation wrought by the huge lead-mining industry of the 18th and 19th centuries. Most of the Yorkshire Dales still bear the scars of this former activity, but Swaledale more than most.

The dale takes its name from the **River Swale** which bubbles into life high on the flanks of High Pike Hill, but only earns its name down in the valley, just above the village of Keld. It careers downhill, leaping over waterfalls at every opportunity, past the villages of **Muker** and **Gunnerside** and catching its breath a little at Reeth. This is the largest village and unofficial capital of Upper Swaledale and Arkengarthdale, sitting as it does at the point where the two valleys meet.

During the next nine miles, the river gets its second wind, speeding up and racing on through the rapids at Marrick Priory to arrive in style at Town Falls in Richmond below the walls of the castle.

SELF-POWERED TRAVEL

CYCLING

I have two measuring scales for the bike-friendliness of an area. Swaledale scores highly on one, absence of traffic, but not on the other, absence of nasty gradients. However, anyone hale and hearty enough to consider riding the **Yorkshire Dales Cycleway** will laugh in the face of hills and this route visits Swaledale. It arrives at Gunnerside via the Oxnop Beck road from Askrigg and returns to Wensleydale from Grinton on the Greets Moss road.

For **road cycling**, Cycle the Dales (www.cyclethedales.org.uk), the cycling arm of the Yorkshire Dales National Park, has turned this section of the big tour into a stand-alone 33-mile day circuit, the Two Valleys Route, along with two others, the 27-mile Swaledale Circular and 52 miles of Tan Hill Toughie. Thankfully for me, and most people I suspect, Cycle the Dales also suggests a gentler family ride in Swaledale. The 15-mile Exploring Swaledale route is actually two loops linked, which could easily be done separately. One loop goes from Gunnerside to Isles Bridge down the main valley road, over the river and back to Gunnerside via Crackpot – five miles and one short steep hill. The other loop links Healaugh, Reeth and Grinton returning on the Harkerside road – seven miles and one not-so-steep hill. I have another favourite road circuit, not official because of one short section off tarmac, but an exhilarating eight miles starting and finishing at one of the best pubs in the dale. From the Punchbowl at Low Row, go over Isles Bridge to Crackpot (get off and push by the waterfalls). Continue uphill to Summer Lodge where the road gives way to a well surfaced track. When you reach tarmac again turn left and enjoy four miles of gentle downhill freewheeling to the main road, then back to the Punchbowl for a well-earned pint.

"Anyone hale and hearty enough to consider riding the Yorkshire Dales Cycleway will laugh in the face of hills."

For **off-road biking**, I reckon that this is the best to be had in the whole of the Dales, because of the huge choice of bridleways and green lanes. Most are remnants from the lead-mining days so are substantial tracks rather than those irritating spectral bridleways – bold green lines on the map that turn out to be imaginary trails in real life, buried under waist-deep heather. Mountain-biking guidebooks abound, with suggested routes; and of course the national park's MTB the Dales web page gives details, including very useful difficulty grades for each section, of two short loops – Booze (10 miles) and Crackpot (15 miles) and one long loop 'The Edge' (24 miles) which can be broken down into short circuits.

If you are a **social biker**, the event for you is on the Spring Bank Holiday weekend every year. The Richmond Meet is a traditional fair, but with a wide variety of cycling events included. Your local contact for all things two-wheeled is the Dales Bike Centre near Reeth (see pages 36 and 175).

WALKING

The **Pennine Way** is the only National Trail to enter Swaledale, and it only just dips its feet in, up at the western end, calling on Thwaite, Keld and Tan Hill.

A much more popular route these days is the **Coast to Coast Walk**, not an official trail but an invention in the 1960s by the inspirational walker and writer Alfred Wainwright. AW, as he is often affectionately known, claimed modestly that he laid a ruler on the map from St Bees in Cumbria to Robin Hood's Bay in the east, and the route almost chose itself. Don't believe a word of it; it could easily have followed Teesdale just to the north or Wensleydale to the south but he deliberately picked Swaledale as the most rewarding walking hereabouts. Unless you are on the full sea-to-sea challenge you're unlikely to want to complete the 30-mile traverse of the dale from Nine Standards Rigg to Richmond, although I do like the idea of following a river from its source. A more practical challenge is perhaps to catch the number 30 bus up the dale and walk back along a section or sections of AW's route. There are a variety of choices: **Keld to Reeth**, 11 miles across the lead-spoil desert of Melbecks Moor; **Keld to Gunnerside**, 6 miles of some of the best riverside walking in the country; **Gunnerside to Reeth**, another lovely

"Inspirational walker and writer Alfred Wainwright deliberately picked Swaledale as the most rewarding walking hereabouts."

ⓘ TOURIST INFORMATION

Reeth Hudson House, The Green ✆ 01748 884059
Richmond Friary Gardens, Victoria Rd ✆ 01748 828742

6 miles, this time along the hillside and through one of Swaledale's few forested areas, Rowleth Wood, an early summer sylvan paradise, with rare lime-loving plants in bloom and warbler song in the air; and **Reeth to Richmond**, ten to11 miles, AW gives a choice of riverside or hillside walking, but both routes take in the ruins of Marrick Priory.

UPPER SWALEDALE

Keld, **Muker** and **Thwaite** form a triumvirate of tiny grey-stone hamlets at the three corners of a triangle, with the isolated hill of Kisdon in the centre. Kisdon is almost an island in fact, being practically surrounded by water; Straw Beck to the south flowing through Muker and the embryonic River Swale hugging its north and east flanks from Keld downstream. Finally, on the western side, a small stream, with the odd name of Skeb Skeugh, wriggles its way through tiny fields and under dry-stone walls to Thwaite. Because of its splendid isolation Kisdon is good walking country, and, weather permitting, you'll always have a panoramic view in one direction or another. Strange then, for such an obvious vantage point, not to have a path to its 1,637-foot summit; last time I was up here, with a walking partner, we both bemoaned the slog through deep heather to reach the cairn (with particularly colourful language on her part). Once there though we revelled in its inaccessibility, sharing a big sky of scudding clouds with no-one but soaring buzzards and passing ravens.

> *"Kidson is good walking country and you'll always have a panoramic view in one direction or another."*

1 KELD

🏠 **Keld Bunkbarn and Yurts** (see page 175)

⛺ **Rukin's Campsite** (see page 176)

For such a small place, the number of buildings barely making double figures, Keld boasts unexpected fame. Its strategic position at the crossing point of the Pennine Way and Coast to Coast Walk helps, but these trails were both deliberately routed here for good reason – the scenic delights of **Keld Gorge** (if you want to make a round walk of it, use the bridleway that rises over Kisdon Hill for the return leg). The River Swale tumbles over a series of waterfalls, Wain Wath Force, Catrake Force and Kisdon

Force among others, beloved of adrenaline kayakers when in spate and wild swimmers at gentler times. Many of these swimmers and paddlers stay in Keld, on the lovely riverside campsite or in the bunkhouse run by the Rukin family at Park House Farm.

From the 1950s Keld was known as a 'dry' village, with the old Cat Hole Inn bought by the Temperance Society and closed – spoilsports! Further bad news in 2006 was the closure of the youth hostel, but this was tempered by its re-opening as a pub/hotel, Keld Lodge: the village is no longer dry.

One building just outside Keld, in a stupendous position gazing down Kisdon Gorge, is **Crackpot Hall**. Originally a shooting lodge, then game keeper's house and finally farm, it ended its occupied life in the 1950s and is now a forlorn but atmospheric ruin.

FOOD & DRINK

Keld Lodge DL11 6LL ☎ 01748 886259 ⊕ www.keldlodge.com. On the top road just out of the village, the old youth hostel is now a hotel with restaurant and bar – effectively the new village pub.

Rukin's Park Lodge Farm DL11 6LJ ☎ 01748 886274 ⊕ www.rukins-keld.co.uk. A village-centre farm providing a-bit-of-everything service, campsite (gloriously cheap and simple by the river), basic groceries and tea shop.

2 MUKER

Muker is the largest of the three villages, with one of my favourite Dales pubs, The Farmers Arms, and a couple of shops. The old vicarage, built in 1680, is a characterful building housing the general store, which also doubles as the village tea shop and tourist information centre. Muker's church, dedicated to St Mary the Virgin, was a welcome arrival, relatively late in the day; until 1580, locals had to carry their dead ten miles along the 'Corpse Road' to Grinton, the nearest consecrated graveyard.

"All the players in Muker Silver band, aged between ten and 70, live in the vicinity of the village, and the community is fiercely proud of its musical ensemble."

Brass-band music has often been a traditional leisure activity in mining communities, and the lead miners of Swaledale were no exception. The miners are long gone but two bands remain in the dale, one in Reeth and the other based here in tiny Muker. All the players in

Muker Silver band, aged between ten and 70, live in the vicinity of the village, and the community is fiercely proud of its musical ensemble. Look out for them at shows and fêtes in the summer, and Christmas carol events as far away as Richmond. They are always high on the bill at Muker show, on the first Wednesday of September, where you will also be entertained by local produce and craft judging, sheepdog trials and fell races.

FOOD & DRINK

Farmers Arms DL11 6QG ℰ 01748 886297 ⌂ www.farmersarmsmuker.co.uk. A really welcoming village local serving Theakstons and a guest beer, and traditional bar snacks.
Muker Village Tea Shop and Stores DL11 6GQ ℰ 01748 886409 ⌂ www.mukervillage. co.uk. Sells a bit of everything, including a range of teas, filter coffee and snacks.

SHOPPING

Swaledale Woollens Strawbeck ℰ 01748 886251 ⌂ www.swaledalewoollens.co.uk. Swaledale and Wensleydale sheep provide the wool to keep the hand-knitting tradition alive, and the garments and rugs created by 30 local knitters are sold here.

3 THWAITE

The tiny hamlet's renown lies in its situation rather than its buildings, and in two celebrity old boys. John Kearton, a 19th-century sheep farmer, had two sons – Richard, and the unusually named Cherry – whose phenomenal natural-history knowledge from an early age was their passport out of their humble-born lives. While 'beating' on a grouse shoot, the young Richard called in a grouse to one of the shooters, and so impressed was the gentleman with the farmer's lad's abilities that he offered him a job where he worked, at Cassell's publishing house in London.

"I think I would have liked a man who refused to wear any suit he would not feel comfortable climbing a tree in."

Cherry later joined his brother, and the two of them went on to have illustrious careers as writers, broadcasters and nature photographers, befriending royalty and American presidents, and inspiring a youthful David Attenborough. Richard was a noted lecturer, so in demand that he could flout normal after-dinner dress codes; I think I would have liked a man who refused to wear any suit he would not feel comfortable climbing a tree in. The brothers are remembered in various local plaques and inscriptions, on their old school in Muker and cottage in Thwaite, and in the name of the Kearton Country Hotel in the village.

The patchwork of fields around Thwaite encompasses some of the most unspoilt, traditional hay meadows in the whole of the dales. The national park rightly prizes them, and the field barns, or 'laithes', that dot the pastoral landscape. They encourage farmers to keep the old ways going, like late hay-cutting (rather than the modern practice of silageing), which encourages a wonderful floral display in June and July, and is a joy to walk around for all but hay-fever sufferers.

"The patchwork of fields encompasses some of the most unspoilt, traditional hay meadows in the whole of the dales."

Thwaite is on one of Swaledale's few links to the outside world, along the road to **Buttertubs Pass**. This strange name refers to caves near the highest point, that either resemble traditional butter containers, or really were used to keep it cool in transit, depending on which old story you choose to believe.

¶¶ FOOD & DRINK

Kearton Country Hotel DL11 6DR ✆ 01748 886277 ⌂ www.keartoncountryhotel.co.uk. A hotel with a tea shop and restaurant attached, open to non-residents.

4 GUNNERSIDE

I had one of those it's-hard-to-imagine moments while basking in the sun, sipping a cup of tea on a bench outside the tea room in Gunnerside. The only sounds were the tinkling of water from the nearby beck, and the odd distant clang of a blacksmith's hammer. Enveloped in this rural comfort blanket, it was indeed astonishing to consider the frantic industrial past of 150 years ago, when Gunnerside was nicknamed Klondike. Some insight into the lead-mining boom can be had in the old smithy, which has operated since 1795, and now doubles as a **museum**. The present blacksmith, Stephen Calvert, is this generation's representative in an unbroken line of six Calvert blacksmiths. Other survivors from the great lead rush are the methodist chapel and the village pub, the Kings Head.

If you follow Gunnerside Beck for a mile or two upstream from the village, you not only are rewarded with a delightful wooded walk, but will get first-hand experience of the impact of past lead-mining in this little valley.

¶¶ FOOD & DRINK

Ghyllfoot Tearooms and Bistro DL11 6LA ✆ 01748 886239 ✆ www.ghyllfoot.co.uk.
A day-time café and evening restaurant, tucked into a corner and selling lead-miners' recipe
cheese cake. The penny-farthing bike over the door was made in the smithy over the road.

SHOPPING

Old Working Smithy and Museum Rose Cottage ✆ 01748 886577. Open in the summer
for a small fee and displaying a fascinating mix of artefacts all originating from the smithy.
Also a working blacksmith's workshop.

5 LOW ROW

Even smaller and quieter than Gunnerside, Low Row is really just a
string of buildings punctuating the main Swaledale Road for mile or
so, three of which are worthy of mention. On
the fell-side above the hamlet, by the side of
the Corpse Road route, sits a little-visited barn
with the uninviting name of the **Dead House**.
In medieval times coffin carriers, on their way
to the church at Grinton, would temporarily
leave their cadaver and nip downhill to
the local ale house for refreshment, before
continuing their solemn journey. We don't
know where Low Row's pub was, or what it was
called, before the 1600s, but from that time it has been the Punchbowl
Inn, next to the church in an area called Feetham.

*"In medieval times
coffin carriers, on
their way to church
at Grinton, would
temporarily leave
their cadaver and
nip downhill to the
local ale house."*

The third building of note here, especially if you have children with
you who need entertaining, is **Hazel Brow Farm** – a working organic
farm where the young (and young at heart) can get up-close to the
animals and follow the nature trail while the grown-ups relax in the café.

¶¶ FOOD & DRINK

Hazel Brow Farm DL11 6NE ✆ 01748 886224 ✆ www.hazelbrow.co.uk. Visitor centre, café,
shop, organic farm produce, walks and children's play area including animal feeding and alpaca
rides. Free entry to café, shop and walks, fee for the rest. Open Easter–Sep except Mon and Fri.
Punch Bowl Inn DL11 6PF ✆ 01748 886233 ✆ www.pbinn.co.uk. The beers here are
well-kept local brews – Theakstons, Black Sheep and Timothy Taylors – but the emphasis is
on food. Meat and game from the dale and fish from Hartlepool are served in the restaurant
that sports a 'Mouseman of Kilburn' carved bar.

MID SWALEDALE: AROUND REETH

6 REETH

Reeth is a Saxon name meaning 'by the stream' which is odd, because it isn't. Two watercourses are not far away though, the River Swale to the south and Arkle Beck to the north draining the valley of Arkengarthdale. Reeth sits strategically between the two valleys, raised safely out of flood range of both boisterous rivers. I like Reeth but it doesn't have the cosy atmosphere of some villages: the village green is disproportionately large, giving the place a spread-out feel.

Reeth was, and still is, the capital of Swaledale, and site of the only market above Richmond, hence the size of the green. The days when the market would fill this space are long gone but one is still held every Friday. All of Reeth's pubs face on to the green and it does well to support three today, but this is nothing compared with the early 1800s at the height of Swaledale's lead-mining boom. Reeth was the centre of the industry and had a staggering ten pubs at the time. The spiritual needs of the miners were met by three chapels, two of which are still open for worship. Reeth has never had its own church, being part of the parish of Grinton with the church a mile away.

"I like Reeth but it doesn't have the cosy atmosphere of some villages: the village green is disproportionately large, giving the place a spread-out feel."

Tourism is by far the biggest employer here now. Virtually every visitor to Swaledale calls in on Reeth and they are well served here by a national park visitor centre, three gift shops, a bookshop, three general stores, and a post office. If you appreciate arts and crafts then carry on up Silver Street from the green and find the **Dales Centre**, a modern set of industrial units which is home to a three-dimensional cross-stitcher, two furniture makers, two sculptors, a jeweller and a worker in stained glass. They produce wonderful work, it's just a shame that the modern centre they are in is so uninspiring. For a little educational entertainment there is a **Swaledale Museum** (✆ 01748 884118 ⌂ www.swaledalemuseum. org) in the old Methodist schoolroom on the corner of the green, a quaint and very traditional local history archive with small shop and café attached.

If you don't need educating or entertaining, just a bench in a quiet corner to sit and muse or read in the sun, then the **Community Orchard Garden** is the place. It's easily found, at the side of the tourist information office, free and accessible to wheelchairs.

Reeth's busiest week of the year is undoubtedly over Whitsun, in late May to early June, when the **Swaledale Festival** (www.swaledale-festival.org.uk) takes place – a celebration of music and the arts.

A waterside wander

Reeth has a wealth of appealing walks, but if you only have time or energy for one it has to be a circular tour of both rivers. First go south from the green to Back Lane, then over the river via the footbridge. Watch sand martins flit in and out of their river bank burrows in summer as you follow the bridleway downstream to Grinton. Here you can resist the temptation to enter the fine Bridge Inn, or not as the case may be. Return to Reeth across the field footpath, diverting up Arkle Beck for a short explore before re-entering the green at its northern end. A delightful 2½-mile easy stroll.

FOOD & DRINK

You won't go hungry or thirsty here; there are six places to get a cup of tea, and a source of freshly baked bread and cakes at **Reeth Bakery** on Silver Street.

Ice Cream Parlour The Green 01748 884929 www.reethicecreamparlour.co.uk. Sixteen flavours of Brymoor ice cream from Jervaulx, or hot drinks for those chilly days.

Overton House Café High Row 01748 884332 www.overtonhousecafe.co.uk. A café in the daytime and restaurant in the evening, very popular, booking required.

Pubs

None of Reeth's three pubs on The Green can really compete with the excellent hostelries in the surrounding villages but it's great that they are all still serving real ale, doing accommodation and thriving in such a small place. They are:

Black Bull Hotel High Row 01748 884213 www.theblackbullreeth.co.uk. Worth a look for its upside-down sign, a gesture of rebellion from a previous landlord to the National Park over a planning dispute.

Buck Hotel DL11 6SW 01748 884210 www.buckhotel.co.uk. Excellent range of real ale and cider. Regular live music.

The Kings Arms High Row 01748 884259 www.thekingsarms.com. Deserves a visit on a cold evening for the fireplace alone, as it must be one of the biggest in the country. When the fire is well banked up the bar feels like a sauna.

7 GRINTON & FREMINGTON

⌂ Dales Bike Centre Fremington (see page 175)

Neither of these neighbouring hamlets has enough to warrant village status today, but an amateur historian will enjoy piecing together jigsaw pieces of a busy and influential past. The bridge linking Grinton and Fremington is at the first point on the River Swale above Richmond where the river could be forded, hence its importance. The oldest evidence is from the Iron Age, with the remains of a fort just east of Grinton by the river, a settlement 1½ miles upstream at Maiden Castle, and boundary earthworks between the two hamlets, blocking the valley bottom completely at one time.

"A maze of footpaths and bridleways links all these places, in a choice of pleasant valley-bottom strolls."

For 400 years St Andrew's Church in **Grinton** was the only one in Upper Swaledale, and had the biggest parish in Yorkshire. This accounts for the size of the building which led to its nickname, 'Cathedral of the Dales'. Although most of the church fabric is now fairly recent, there are fragments of the original Norman church, built by the monks of Bridlington Priory, a long way from home. Bats inhabit the church, both real pipistrelles in the roof space, and striking copper sculptures hanging from the walls, courtesy of Michael Kusz from the Dales Centre Studios in Reeth.

More recent, but still old and interesting, buildings are **Fremington corn mill**, with a rare wooden waterwheel, **Grinton Lodge**, once a shooting lodge but now a youth hostel, and the village pub.

A maze of footpaths and bridleways links all these places, in a choice of pleasant valley-bottom strolls, but two obvious higher-level walks also warrant a try: **Fremington Edge** on the north side of the valley, and **High Harker Hill** on the Grinton side. Another alternative is to hire bikes from the Dales Bike Centre and go for a pedal.

⦀ FOOD & DRINK

Bridge Inn Grinton ☎ 01748 884224 ⌂ www.bridgeinn-grinton.co.uk. A 13th-century coaching inn, well-loved by locals and visitors. Food is high quality and often includes game shot by the landlord. Unusually, the beer is Jennings from Cumbria, but a local guest ale often accompanies it. Day fishing licences and rods for hire behind the bar.

CYCLE HIRE & REPAIR

Dales Bike Centre Fremington ✆ 01748 884908 🖱 www.dalesbikecentre.co.uk. An old barn converted to everything two-wheeled. Road and mountain bikes for hire, bike shop, service and repair, bike wash and showers (not just for riders, sweaty walkers as well). Snacks and drinks are on the menu in an attached café and bunk and breakfast accommodation is also available. All in all a very handy facility, and not just for bikers.

8 ARKENGARTHDALE

If the name of the valley itself isn't eccentric enough, then what about some of the places in it? Booze, Whaw, Raw and Faggergill could easily have been words picked at random for their comedy value. Arkle Town sounds as if it should be the largest settlement here, but there is virtually nothing of it; that title goes to the compact village of **Langthwaite**, straddling Arkle Beck with a graceful, stone, arched bridge that featured in the TV series *All Creatures Great and Small*.

"Right on top of the moor, the Tan Hill Inn materialises out of the cloud, mist or snow. At 1,732 feet above sea level it is the highest pub in Britain."

The lower dale is surprisingly lush and wooded for Swaledale, but if you travel up the valley on the road towards Brough, the landscape turns much less cultivated and more open. Just beyond the head of the dale, and right on top of the moor, where the words wild and bleak usually apply, a most unexpected sight materialises out of the cloud, mist or snow – an inn, the Tan Hill Inn to be precise, at 1,732 feet above sea level the highest pub in Britain (and one of the most remote from other habitation, too).

ⵏⵏ FOOD & DRINK

Charles Bathurst Inn Langthwaite DL11 6EN ✆ 01748884567 🖱 www.cbinn.co.uk. A large roadside inn named after the local lord of the manor and lead mine owner. CB Inn, as it's known, is friendly and popular, valued for its cask beer from Black Sheep, Theakstons and Timothy Taylors, extensive wine cellar and very good food. Meat and game are all sourced from Swaledale.

Red Lion Inn Langthwaite DL11 6RE ✆ 01748 884218 🖱 www.langthwaite.free-online. co.uk. A marvellous, atmospheric little village local, almost as different to the CB Inn as you could get. Black Sheep beer, hot drinks, local honey and preserves and bar snacks, but nowhere near the emphasis on food of its near neighbour.

LIVING OFF THE LAND

This is not arable country. 'Beasts' (to use a fine Yorkshire-ism) are the lifeblood of the Dales – cattle in the valleys and sheep on the fells, all tended lovingly by hardy Yorkshire farmers.

1 Sheep huddled together on Sheep Day at Skipton. (WTY) 2 Wensleydale Creamery: where all that Dales milk goes. (SS) 3 Limestone beef on the hoof. (YDNPA)

STREETLIFE IN THE DALES

There may be a bustle to these towns but they are still old, full of tradition and 'Slow' in the nicest possible way. You won't find many supermarkets but you will enjoy the butchers, bakers and candlestick makers.

1 Richmond town and that imposing castle keep. (wty) 2 Main Street, Pateley Bridge. (ss)
3 Valley Gardens: the most famous of Harrogate's 11 public gardens. (wty) 4 Ripon's
horn-blower sounds his daily blast. (ss) 5 Knaresborough viaduct crosses the River Nidd. (ss)
6 Quality teas in Harrogate at Bettys, a Yorkshire institution. (ss)

THERE'S NOWT SO QUEER AS DALES FOLK

You won't have to dig too deep to unearth the quirky and eccentric in this part of the world. Sometimes it's out there 'bold as brass' as they say.

1 *Trompe-l'œil*: not a real door but a wall painting in Knaresborough. (CM) 2 The 'welcoming' entrance to the Forbidden Corner. (WTY) 3 Sheep racing at the annual Masham Sheep Fair. (PMY/A)

THE NOT-SO-FAMOUS GROUSE

It's 05.45 on a cold April morning and I'm not tucked up in bed but huddled in a wall corner of an old sheep-shelter in Arkengarthdale. I'm wearing most of the clothes I possess, a woolly hat down over the ears and sporting a drip on the end of my nose. Why? I hear you ask. Well, following a tip-off from a bird-watching friend, I'm in the right place to wait for dawn to break and witness a unique stage show. Two of the players are already here. I can see them through a convenient hole in the wall, on a stage of short cropped grass surrounded by tussocky rushes and heather. As the morning brightens, colour washes into the landscape and I can make out detail in the birds. They are the size and shape of small chickens, very dark with intense red eyebrows – they are male black grouse or moorcocks (*Tetrao tetrix*).

The two birds are suddenly joined by a third which struts into the arena and spreads its tail to reveal a white pompom of feathers beneath. He opens his mouth and, in a bubble of warm misty breath, produces a bizarre series of indignant burbles and hisses aimed at the other two males, who reply in a similar fashion. What I was witnessing was a communal courtship display called a 'lek' which is performed by black grouse and only two other species of bird in Britain.

By the time I'd seen enough and slunk away downhill out of sight, six males were giving it what for, and an audience of female grey hens was watching from the periphery, selecting their preferred mate – presumably the most impressive strutter and burbler.

What makes this seem doubly special is its increasing rarity. The black grouse is in serious decline nationally: Swaledale's is the most southerly population in England and the only one in Yorkshire. Since 1996 a consortium of interested parties, including the RSPB, Natural England and shooting organisations, have initiated the Black Grouse Recovery Project for the north Pennines. Their main push is on habitat improvement, reducing sheep grazing on moor edges and encouraging traditional hay meadows, and it seems to be working.

In an inspired move they have also managed to recruit the help of Famous Grouse whisky who have produced a new blend, which incorporates the aromatic peatiness of Islay malt. It's already got rave reviews and is selling well, with 50p from every bottle going to the recovery project. So, if you want to help, go and search out this new whisky and buy a bottle, or ask for it by name at the pub. What's it called? The Black Grouse, of course.

9 TAN HILL INN

DL11 6ED 01833 628246 www.tanhillinn.co.uk. See also *Accommodation*, page 175

I'll ask the obvious question. Why would anyone in their right mind build a pub up here, on an extraordinarily remote junction of roads on the moors northwest of Arkengarthdale? Coal, is the short answer.

The black stuff has been dug out of the ground on Tan Hill since the 12th century, and remnants of the pits, shafts and quarries still dot the moorland around the inn. The current 17th-century building replaced an earlier one which catered to the miners' needs in this lonely spot, and has been here ever since.

"This is a place full of character, almost a world apart. A roaring fire warms the bar, though access is often blocked by the resident cats and dogs, and sometimes even sheep, toasting themselves by the hearth."

The last mine closed in 1929, but the pub managed to keep going because of its high-altitude fame, and more passing trade began in 1965 on the opening of the Pennine Way footpath, which goes right past the front door. Television adverts for double glazing, an annual sheep show in May, and regular live folk and rock music have kept people making the pilgrimage up the hill. Is it worth it? Absolutely: this is a place full of character, almost a world apart.

More often than not, a roaring fire warms the bar, which is a comfort if you can get close to it – access is often blocked by the resident cats and dogs, and sometimes even sheep, toasting themselves by the hearth. If you come in winter, be prepared for a long stay, as the pub can be cut off for weeks on end after heavy snow, and consequently has its own caterpillar-tracked snowmobile.

10 MARRICK

What is now a favoured haunt for white-water canoeists and kayakers was obviously once likewise for builders of monasteries, because two are here, one on either side of the river. The remains of **Ellerton Priory**, constructed in the late 12th century for Cistercian nuns, were incorporated into a Victorian shooting lodge which is now a private house on the south bank of the river. Nearby, but on the opposite side of the river, were the Benedictine nuns at **Marrick Priory**. I like to imagine those medieval ladies dressed in different coloured habits, waving to each other across the rapids. Not surprisingly, considering its position, Marrick Priory is now an outdoor education centre (but still owned by the Church of England). While it caters mainly for groups of schoolchildren, the centre's instructors and equipment can be hired for a day or half day. **Marrick village** lies about half a mile up the hillside, at the top end of a very pleasant walk through Steps Wood.

LOWER SWALEDALE: INCLUDING RICHMOND

The scenery is still exquisite here; **Richmond** itself is handily placed for walks into the dale, with paths along the valley and high up along the level-topped cliff of Whitcliffe Scar.

11 RICHMOND

🏠 **Culloden Tower** and **Old Cello Workshop** (see page 175)

This isn't just Richmond, this is *the* Richmond – the one that all 56 others worldwide are named after, including its more well-known Surrey counterpart and far bigger sister in Virginia, USA. The name is pure French, Riche Mont meaning Strong Hill, and refers to the defensive site the Norman **castle** is built upon, high above a loop in the river and still massively imposing.

The Swale has made no concessions to civilisation; it is still wild and frisky, plunging over the spectacular cascade of **Town Falls**, directly below the castle. Riverside Road follows its northern bank and is a lovely place to walk, cycle, picnic or paddle, but take note of the signs warning of dangerous, fast-rising water levels at times.

"All roads seem to lead to the cobbled marketplace and it does take your breath away when you emerge into it as it is enormous – one of the largest in the country."

In the town centre, all roads seem to lead to the cobbled **marketplace**, and it does take your breath away when you emerge into it as it is enormous – one of the largest in the country. Prince Charles was certainly taken with it, likening it to the grand Tuscan piazza of Siena in Italy. On most days this exotic ambience is not obvious as the marketplace doubles as a large free car park, but empty it is impressive, and at its very best on Saturdays when the big market takes place. The third Saturday of the month is particularly good as it also incorporates a farmers' market.

North of the marketplace modern Richmond begins to intrude, but there are three places to seek out, the **Georgian Theatre Royal**, the **Richmondshire Museum**, and the **Friary Gardens**. Where the green space of the last of these is now was once the site of an old Franciscan Friary and it still retains the statuesque ruins of an old bell tower, and a monastic sense of peace and serenity. There's also a good deal of conspicuously handsome **Georgian streetscape**, in Newbiggin Broad and elsewhere, and some alluring back alleys, or **wynds**, such as Cornforth Hill, leading steeply down through two of the surviving town gateways.

For some strange reason Richmond town does not venture south of the river at all, the only building of note on this side being the **old railway station**. The rest remains as park or farmland, ideal country for walking, with grandstand views of the castle in the old town. An upstream stroll takes you on to the roundhouse nature trails, a series of scenic woodland loops, linked to make one four-mile walk, or individual shorter circular walks. If you head in the other direction from town, one mile downstream you will find the riverside ruins of Easby Abbey, and a return path on the other side of the river following the old railway line. This route is called the Drummer Boy Walk (see box, below). For exploring the town itself on foot, three very good town trails are available free online (⌖ www.richmond.org) or from the tourist information centre.

"The rest of Richmond remains as park or farmland, ideal country for walking, with grandstand views of the castle in the old town."

It's no surprise that Richmond is the cultural centre of Richmondshire (an old un-official fiefdom and now a district council area), and it hosts a wealth of regular events throughout the year. If you want peace and

THE RICHMOND DRUMMER BOY

I can remember being told this story as a child and hoping that it wasn't true, the horror of a solitary underground death filling my young mind with nightmares. It's said that soldiers in Richmond Castle chanced upon a small hole in a cellar wall which seemed to continue as a passage. It was too narrow for an adult to enter so they sent in a young drummer boy, complete with drum, to explore. He was instructed to bang his drum as he walked so the soldiers could track his progress by listening above ground. They followed the faint drumbeats across the marketplace and Frenchgate towards Easby Abbey for half a mile when the sound suddenly stopped. The unfortunate boy was never heard or seen again but a stone was laid at the point where the drumming was last heard, and it can still be seen in a field at the end of Easby Wood. Ghostly subterranean drumming can also be heard on still evenings … in my nightmares at least.

quiet you had best avoid them, but if you want lively entertainment then time your visit for two in particular. **The Richmond Meet** is an annual fair, with floats, parades, cycle events and general carnival atmosphere, held over the Spring Bank Holiday weekend; and during the last week in September the **Richmond Walking and Book Festival** (⌂ www. booksandboots.org) features guided walks for all abilities during the days, and evening events to celebrate the written word.

Richmond Castle

Riverside Rd ✆ 01748 822493; English Heritage.

Few towns are more dominated by their castle than Richmond, partly because the town is relatively small but also because this is a genuinely impressive building. The 100-foot-high keep towers over everything and, in my opinion, provides a viewpoint from the top to equal any in Yorkshire. Swaledale snakes away westwards while to the east lies the flat Cleveland plain laid out like a green patchwork quilt, with industrial Teeside hinted at in the distance.

Back in 1066 William the Conqueror had a dilemma. He was now boss of a lot of foreigners in their own country who didn't like him. His strategy was to delegate – allocate big chunks of land to his trusted earls and barons and let them control the resident Anglo-Saxons. His cousin Alan Rufus was given this corner of North Yorkshire and he must have had a healthy respect for the locals as he immediately set to building a castle on a 'strong hill' to defend himself. Most of the other Norman lords started with a temporary wooden fort, but Alan went for stones straightaway, making Richmond castle the equal-oldest stone Norman castle in England with those in Durham and Colchester. Big as it is, the castle was once even more extensive as it included what is now the marketplace within its walls. During the 14th-century worries about Scottish invasion, the town populace was allowed behind the protective outer bailey which stood where the crescent of market-side Georgian buildings is now. When the Scots danger passed, the bailey was gradually dismantled leaving the marketplace as part of the town and not the castle. This explains the odd position of the castle chapel, Trinity Church, outside the walls; it now houses the **Green Howards Museum**.

"The 100-foot-high keep towers over everything and provides a viewpoint from the top to equal any in Yorkshire."

English Heritage charge a reasonable entry fee into the castle and it is money well spent; you can access walkways around the walls, a small museum and a shop, but the keep alone is worth the fee. Don't neglect the outside of the building either. If anything I think this is even more interesting than inside.

Richmondshire Museum

Ryder's Wynd ✆ 01748 825611 🖰 www.richmondshiremuseum.org.uk; Apr–Oct daily.
This small local history museum tucked away in Ryder's Wynd near the tourist information office covers life as it was in Richmond and Swaledale in a gentle, traditional style. No touch-screen virtual experiences here or even audio-visual presentations, just artefacts, models and reconstructions. Subjects covered include lead mining, a village post office, a town chemist's shop, toys through the ages and, of course, a set from the ever popular TV series *All Creatures Great and Small*, based on the life of vet James Herriot, who lived and worked in this area.

Green Howards Museum

Trinity Church Sq ✆ 01748 826561 🖰 www.greenhowards.org.uk; closed Sun; children free.
The Green Howards Regiment has been in existence since 1688, but has only been based in Richmond since 1873. The unusual name originates from an early Regimental Colonel, Charles Howard of Castle Howard fame, but as another Howards Regiment existed at the time, they had to distinguish between the two. Based on colour of uniforms the Green Howards and the Buff Howards were born.

Many of the Green Howards were killed in World War I, after which a number of their private memorabilia collections were sent to the regiment. The collections of mainly medals and uniforms were housed in barrack rooms, huts and sheds from 1922 until the empty Holy Trinity Church came up for sale in 1970. If you have a military background or Green Howard connections then you will love this place but for others like me who have neither, it risks being very stuffy. The Museum Trust realised this and have worked hard on much-needed modernisation recently. Popular new additions are the Kidzone where children can dress up (always a winner) and the Family History Research Centre.

"Popular new additions are the Kidzone where children can dress up (always a winner) and the Family History Research Centre."

The Georgian Theatre Royal

Victoria St ✆ 01748 823710 ⌂ www.georgiantheatreroyal.co.uk; hourly tours, six days a week during daytime for much of the year.

My choice of production was *A Midsummer Night's Dream* by Bill the Bard or *Bouncers and Shakers*, a 1980s-style comedy with a warning about strong language. I suppose I should have gone traditional when visiting the country's oldest surviving Georgian Theatre building but I never could resist a John Godber play (and he is from Yorkshire). The show was brilliant, well directed and acted, with the character of the venue adding to the experience. This is a wonderful place, part Grade 1 listed building, part museum, but also a very busy working theatre.

"I suppose I should have gone traditional when visiting the country's oldest surviving Georgian Theatre, but the show was brilliant; well directed and acted, with the character of the venue adding to the experience."

It was built in 1788 at the height of Richmond's heyday by actor/manager Samuel Butler, but, faced with dwindling performances, closed in 1848. Miraculously the buildings were still intact in the 1960s when a group of local campaigners formed a non-profit trust and the theatre re-opened. Although the facilities were extended in 2003, the auditorium remains unchanged and still only has a capacity of 214 in a sunken pit, boxes on three sides and a gallery. It is quaint, intimate, authentic and as far removed from a modern concert arena as you could get, and I loved it. So did Cathy and Graham, the couple sitting next to us. 'We come here at least once a month, sometimes twice in the same week. There's all sorts on – comedy club last week, that was good, rock music tribute bands, Shakespeare, lots of jazz evenings next month. We don't really mind what we see; it's the place we love. The "Poetry and Pints" evenings in the bar we always come to because they are free and next week is Museum Week where they convert everything back to its 1788 state, candlelight, wooden benches, hand painted scenery, Georgian costumes, the lot – it's great.'

Richmond's Old Railway Station

Station Rd ✆ 01748 850123 ⌂ www.richmondstation.com.

Richmond's old railway terminus, or 'The Station' as it is known, is probably busier now than it ever was when trains arrived daily from Darlington and beyond.

This building has a very special place in the Richmond community's heart; the local people fought tooth and nail to keep the railway open in the 1960s but lost out in the end. Their successors, and maybe some of the original activists, formed the Richmondshire Building Preservation Trust in 2003 and have steered the project that has produced this cultural centre. I like the fact that they have not forgotten the building's roots; the railway theme is everywhere, with evocative black-and-white images of steam locomotives, and a heritage centre devoted to rail memorabilia.

"I like the fact that they have not forgotten the building's roots; the railway theme is everywhere, with evocative images and a heritage centre devoted to rail memorabilia."

Hundreds of people a day pass through the doors to visit the cinema, café-restaurant, art gallery or heritage centre and many, myself included, leave with bags laden with goodies produced on-site by five artisan food makers every day except Mondays (see page 105).

¶¶ FOOD & DRINK

I've covered places to eat and drink in town, at the Old Railway Station and out of town separately. For its size Richmond is a little disappointing on the gastronomic front but there are exceptions. I wouldn't particularly recommend any town pubs for eating but the two listed (Bishop Blaize and Ralph Fitz Randal) would suit fussy beer drinkers.

Richmond town

Bishop Blaize Market Pl ✆ 01748 823065. A busy town centre pub in a very old building. Wide choice of beers.

Cross View Tea Rooms Market Pl ✆ 01748 825897. This place is always busy, which has to be a good sign. Prices are very reasonable and although the coffee is nothing special, the fresh cakes are.

Frenchgate 29 Café Frenchgate ✆ 01748 826669. A bistro-style café with a reputation for good food and friendly and helpful service.

Frenchgate Restaurant Frenchgate ✆ 01748 822087 ⌂ www.thefrenchgate.co.uk. This is the place in Richmond to get dressed up and treat yourself if you are into fashionable European cuisine. The food is excellent, but expect your wallet to be a lot lighter when you leave. Open every lunchtime and evening.

Ralph Fitz Randal Queens Rd ✆ 01748 828080 ⌂ www.jdwetherspoon.co.uk. A former post office given the Wetherspoon treatment and turned into a rather cavernous pub. That said, with six cask ales on tap at any given time you may not notice the décor.

Rustique Chantry Wynd ✆ 01748 821565 🖰 www.rustiqueyork.co.uk. A sister restaurant to Rustique in York with the quality just as high. The meals are French-influenced and served in a lively bistro atmosphere.

Richmond Old Station

The Angel's Share Bakery and Pasta Shop ✆ 01748 828261. Heavenly breads, quiches, terrines, tarts and cakes baked daily, plus homemade pasta.

Archers Jersey Dairy Ice Cream ✆ 01748 850123 🖰 www.archersjerseyicecream.com. John and Susan Archer made a bold move when they lost their Friesian dairy herd to foot-and-mouth disease. They replaced it with a herd of Jersey cattle and decided to make ice cream. The rich creamy milk is brought straight from the farm to the parlour in the station and made into a bewildering array of flavours … you think of it, they've probably got it.

Lacey's Cheese ✆ 01748 828264 🖰 www.laceyscheese.co.uk. They say cheese makes you dream. Simon Lacey learned the craft of cheese making at the Swaledale Cheese Company but dreamt of running his own cheese-making business, and here it is. The cheeses are all handmade using traditional methods and locally sourced products (the Swaledale beer in the ale cheese couldn't be more local), both natural rind and hand-waxed varieties, smoked, matured or flavoured.

Richmond Brewing Company ✆ 01748 828266 🖰 www.richmondbrewing.co.uk. The brewer Nick Elliot produces three different ales as I write: Richmond Station Ale (light and golden), Stump Cross Ale (rich and dark) and Swale (smooth session beer). Look out for them as guest beers in pubs or bottles over the counter here at the brewery.

Velvet Heaven ✆ 01748 825340 🖰 www.velvetheaven.co.uk. Homemade confectionary with a particular emphasis on fudge.

Out of town

For quieter drinking and food worth travelling for, two country pubs to the north of Richmond stand out.

Shoulder of Mutton Kirby Hill DL11 7JH ✆ 01748 822772 🖰 www.shoulderofmutton.net. Attractive ivy-fronted building in the centre of the village with views of Ravensworth Castle. Excellent food Wed–Sun; excellent beer all the time.

White Swan Inn Gilling West DL10 5JG ✆ 01748 821123. A very lively, welcoming village local in a 17th-century building with a resident ghost called Jack. There are always two guest micro-brewery beers on sale plus Black Sheep; this is one of their select 'flagsheep' pubs. Food is locally sourced, traditional and good value.

12 EASBY ABBEY

DL10 7JU; free, English Heritage.

Easby is a tiny hamlet perched on the banks of the Swale, three-quarters of a mile downstream from Richmond, and home to this substantial and atmospheric ruin. Historians always suspected that Easby had been a Christian site long before the abbey was built, and this was confirmed in 1931 when pieces of ancient stone carvings were found built into the walls of the church. When pieced back together they re-formed a magnificent 8th-century English cross, now in London's Victoria and Albert Museum. The dedication of the church to St Agatha was also a clue as her cult was a very early one, at its peak when Christianity first came to Britain. Poor old St Agatha, by the way, was tortured in life by having her breasts cut off and presented to her on a platter. A superficial similarity in shape led to the ignominy of her becoming the patron saint of bakers and bell makers. Recently, and I think a touch more respectfully, she has been venerated as patron saint of breast cancer patients.

"Historians always suspected that Easby had been a Christian site long before the abbey was built, and this was confirmed in 1931 when pieces of ancient stone carvings were found built into the walls of the church."

The present church was rebuilt in 1152 at the same time as the abbey by the 'White Canons' of the Premonstratensian order, who decorated it with colourful frescoes. Some of these survived the Reformation by being whitewashed and are now re-exposed in these more liberal times.

The history of the abbey has run along the same lines as many other Yorkshire abbeys: 12th century founding on land donated by the local Norman lord, 300 years of power and influence followed by an abrupt end with Henry VIII's dissolution of the monasteries. A common practice at this time was for valuable relics in the abbey to be re-used by the, now new, Anglican churches. Easby Abbey's bell and choir stalls found their way into St Mary's Church in Richmond and are still there.

UPDATES WEBSITE

You can post your comments and recommendations, and read the latest feedback and updates from other readers online at www.bradtupdates.com/yorkshiredales.

40 Years of Pioneering Publishing

In 1974, Hilary Bradt took a road less travelled and published her first travel guide, written whilst floating down the Amazon.

40 years on and a string of awards later, Bradt has a list of 200 titles, including travel literature, Slow Travel guides and wildlife guides. And our pioneering spirit remains as strong as ever – we're happy to say there are still plenty of roads less travelled to explore!

Bradt ...take the road less travelled

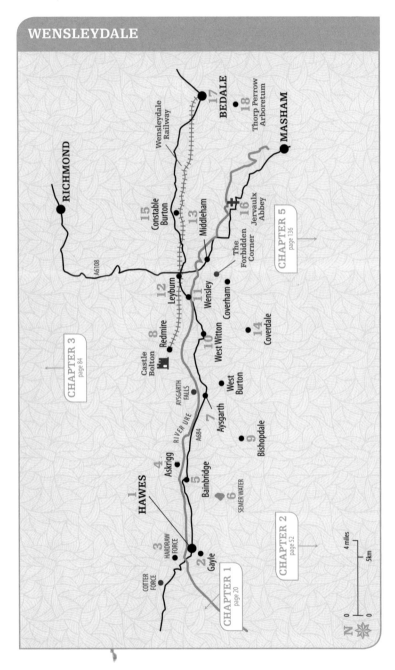

RICHMOND

BEDALE

MASHAM

Wensleydale Railway

Thorp Perrow
Arboretum

15
Constable
Burton

13
Middleham

A6108

The Forbidden
Corner

16
Jervaulx
Abbey

CHAPTER 5
page 136

12
Leyburn

11
Wensley

Coverham

CHAPTER 3
page 84

8
Redmire

10
West Witton

14
Coverdale

Castle
Bolton

AYSGARTH
FALLS

West
Burton

RIVER URE

7
Aysgarth

9
Bishopdale

A684

4
Askrigg

5
Bainbridge

1
HAWES

6
SEMER WATER

3
HARDRAW
FORCE

2
Gayle

COTTER
FORCE

CHAPTER 1
page 20

CHAPTER 2
page 52

N

0   4 miles
0   5km

4
WENSLEYDALE

'This is in most places waste, solitary, unpleasant, unsightly, mute and still.' Poor old William Camden didn't much enjoy his visit to Wensleydale in 1590. We tend to place more value on wilderness today, so much so that this valley is one of the most popular tourist destinations in Yorkshire, and in peak holiday season at least you would have to work hard to find the 'solitary, mute and still' elements. The main valley is the longest of the Yorkshire Dales, and, oddly, named after one of its smaller villages rather than its river, the Ure. A busy 'A' road runs most of its length, linking the bustling towns of **Hawes, Leyburn**, **Middleham** and **Bedale**, and honeypot villages of **Bainbridge** and **Aysgarth**. Wensleydale has a fascinating history and bags of charm; a visit to the museum at Hawes can give you an excellent insight into the area's past, and traditions from quieter times. To escape the crowds try heading away from the valley-bottom roads, up the fell-sides or into one of the tributary side valleys like **Coverdale**, **Bishopdale** or **Raydale**. Alternatively, visit the main valley at off-peak times, especially after heavy rain when its many spectacular waterfalls are at their best.

> *"We tend to place more value on wilderness today, so much so that this valley is one of the most popular tourist destinations in Yorkshire."*

SELF-POWERED TRAVEL
CYCLING
One long-distance road route, the **Yorkshire Dales Cycleway**, nips into Wensleydale at Hawes and then out again from Askrigg over into Swaledale, returning lower down and running the full length of Coverdale.

The national park's **Cycle the Dales** website (⌂ www.cyclethedales.org.uk) features three day rides that traverse a section of Wensleydale then cross the hills to either Swaledale (33 miles), Wharfedale (45 miles) or the Eden Valley via Tan Hill (52 miles). These are long and hilly routes for fit and experienced bikers only. The website does not list any **easier rides** for families or less masochistic folk, and I would take issue with this as I think some perfectly suitable rides exist. The trick is to avoid the main A684 of course, and this can be done almost completely in a nine-mile circuit taking in Askrigg, Thornton Rust, Aysgarth, Carperby and Woodhall. One or two short, steep sections keep you warm and the roads are relatively quiet. Other very short but highly scenic circular rides include Lower Coverdale – where you could join up Coverham, West Scrafton, Carlton (six miles) – and Raydale from Bainbridge via Marsett and Stalling Busk (seven miles).

In Lower Wensleydale where the hills settle down into hummocks, a triangle of land between Leyburn, Bedale and Masham contains a network of very quiet minor roads – excellent gentle biking country. Those lovely people at the Wensleydale Railway allow bikes on the train for free so you could take a one-way rail journey from Bedale to Redmire, then make up your own route back on little roads for 20 miles or as far as you fancy, and hop on the train further down the line.

For **mountain bikes**, Wensleydale is as good as anywhere in the Dales. The **MTB the Dales** section of the national park website recommends two long and difficult routes; a circuit of Dodd Fell (18 miles) and a tour of Mid Wensleydale from Aysgarth (21 miles). Way too far for my delicate rear on rocky tracks; my favourite shorter routes are from West Burton (go east on Morpeth Gate green lane to Witton Steeps, down the road to West Witton and return via Green Gate green lane; six miles) and from Bainbridge (up to Stake Allotments via High Lane and Busk Lane tracks; ten miles, half on tarmac and half on gravel).

HORSERIDING

There are two venues in or around the dale where someone else's horse can do your walking for you:

RIDING CENTRES

Masham Riding and Trekking Centre Swinton, Masham ✆ 01765 689636 or 01765 689241 🖱 www.mashamridingcentre.com. Treks of various length, and lessons for all ages.
Wensleydale Equestrian Gill Edge, Bainbridge ✆ 01969 650367 🖱 www.
wensleydaletrekking.co.uk. Trekking for all sizes and abilities, as well as riding lessons.

WALKING

One official long-distance **National Trail** flirts with Wensleydale. In its upper reaches it is crossed at Hawes by the Pennine Way on its way from Fountains Fell to Great Shunner Fell. Hawes is also on the route of an unofficial circular trail of 55 miles, a traverse of both Wensleydale and Swaledale, called the **Herriot Way**. Elsewhere, the 24 miles of dale, daleside, and side dales offer a plethora of full- and part-day walks to suit almost everyone. I say 'almost' because those of you searching for the high peaks won't find them here. Wensleydale's hills aren't as extrovertly obvious as the Three Peaks or Wharfedale Fells so consequently don't draw the crowds. These are my sort of hills – empty ones.

The best highish-level walks I think, are Pennhill Beacon above West Witton, Wether Fell from Hawes and a short, sharp pull to the summit of Addlebrough near Bainbridge. Upstream of West Burton is the hidden, unnamed valley containing Walden Beck with two short roads that lead in and suddenly stop. During all my time in this secluded corner I have never seen another visiting walker, just farmers going about their business. Cotterdale near Hawes and Hardraw is a similar quiet idyll.

UPPER WENSLEYDALE: HAWES, GAYLE & HARDRAW

1 HAWES

Sitting at the meeting point of at least four ancient packhorse routes, Hawes is undoubtedly the capital of Upper Wensleydale and its position far up the dale makes it the highest-altitude market town in Yorkshire. Its popularity has waxed and waned over the years: booms with the building of the Lancaster–Richmond turnpike road and the coming of the railway in the 1870s, slumps when the mills went quiet, and on the railways closure in the 1960s. Hawes is now busier than it ever has been but ironically, the tourists that the town almost completely depends on are visiting to celebrate many of its old industries: cheese production, textile weaving and rope making.

"If you want to see Hawes at its vibrant best then go on a Tuesday. This is the day of the street stall-market and the livestock auction mart, always an entertaining, multi-sensory experience."

The **Wensleydale Creamery** is probably Hawes's busiest attraction but visitors also flock to the old railway station where the national park has a **visitor centre** with the hugely absorbing **Dales Countryside Museum** attached (01969 666239). You can spend an entertaining and informative couple of hours here, without noticing the passing of time. It's more a celebration of family life in the country than a set of this-is-what-happened-here displays. Cheese and butter making, sheep farming, lead mining and hand knitting are all brought to life by an outstanding collection of local bygones and domestic objects gathered from all over the Dales. It amply justifies the entrance fee, especially for children, who get in free, and will really enjoy the hands-on displays and dressing-up opportunities.

The shops and businesses of Hawes are a nice mix, with butchers, electrical stores, grocers and hardware shops catering for the locals but also the expected wealth of outdoor gear, gift and craft shops, and numerous cafés of course. One place that manages to hit both markets is **The Ropemakers** at the east end of town, and talking of markets, if you want to see Hawes at its vibrant best then go on a Tuesday outside of school holidays. This is the day of the street stall-market and the livestock auction mart, always an entertaining, multi-sensory experience.

Wensleydale Creamery

Gayle Lane 01969 667664 www.wensleydale.co.uk.

Lovers of real Wensleydale cheese have some unlikely benefactors to thank: the French, a local farmer called Kit Calvert and two Plasticine heroes in the form of Wallace and Gromit.

The recipe for this mild, white cow's-milk cheese almost certainly came over from France with the Cistercian monks and was passed down via farmers' wives, to the dairy at Hawes. Twice in the last 80 years this sole producer of genuine from-the-dale Wensleydale cheese almost closed. The first time, in the 1930s depression, local farmers rallied around one of their own, Kit Calvert, who called the meeting in the town hall and bullied enough support to keep the dairy running. On the next occasion in 1992 the then owners, Dairy Crest, actually closed the dairy and had the effrontery to move production to Lancashire. A team of ex-managers bought the building and opened it under the name of Wensleydale Creamery, but making it a going concern wasn't easy. The breakthrough came when, in *A Close Shave*, one of Nick Park's inimitable Wallace and Gromit animations, Wallace uttered the immortal words 'Not even Wensleydale!' when he finds his lady friend doesn't like cheese and the creamery's steady business exploded. The visitor centre (☎ 01969 667664 🖰 www.wensleydale.co.uk) now entertains 200,000 people a year who enjoy the 'cheese experience' tour, explore the museum, eat in the restaurant or just select gifts from the now huge selection of branded cheeses and Wallace and Gromit memorabilia in the shop.

The Ropemakers

Town Foot ☎ 01969 667487 🖰 www.ropemakers.co.uk.

The Outhwaite family have been making ropes in Hawes since 1905 and on the present Town Foot site from the 1920s. In the early days ropes made from hemp, flax, jute and cotton were taken around the Dales by Mr Outhwaite's personal horse and cart. Most of the Swaledale, Wharfedale and Wensleydale farmers in particular relied on Outhwaite's ropes for sale at weekly markets; such was the well-earned reputation the family developed that their nearest serious competitor was 35 miles away in Lancaster.

"The business passed from father to son through the 20th century and is a working ropery that still supplies ropes to farms and industry."

The business passed from father to son through the 20th century, moving with the times by installing electric power for the twisting machine in the 1950s and using manmade fibres for the first time in the 1960s. In the 1970s Tom Outhwaite was ready to retire but, with no family successor to take over, the enterprise was bought by Peter and Ruth Annison. To this day they carry on the Outhwaite traditions, under the old family name. This is a working ropery that still supplies ropes to farms and industry, but the Annisons were astute enough to realise that people will pay to be hypnotised by the fascinating rope-making process. Hour-long guided tours for groups are available but I was happy enough just to wander around and have a nosy, which is free of charge. There is a lot to entertain and inform, including knot boards where visitors are invited to try their hand at fancy knot tying.

¶¶ FOOD & DRINK

Not counting pubs, there are ten places in Hawes where a brew and a snack can be had and to be honest I could quite happily recommend any of them. Whittling the list down to three, my favourite take-away, pub and café are:

The Chippie Market Pl ✆ 01969 667663. Friendly and good value to eat in or out.
The Crown Market Pl ✆ 01969 667212 ⁷ www.crownhawes.co.uk. A good range of Theakstons beers plus guests, high quality traditional pub grub and good value B&B.
Herriot's Kitchen Main St ✆ 01969 667536 ⁷ www.herriotsinhawes.co.uk. Not just a café but an art gallery offering painting courses; B&B.

2 GAYLE

This hamlet owes its existence to one building, not a church or castle for a change, but a mill. **Gayle Mill** (✆ 01969 667320 ⁷ www.gaylemill. org.uk) is the oldest virtually unaltered cotton mill in the world. It was built here in 1784 by the Routh brothers, two canny entrepreneurs who saw the business opportunities the new turnpike road would bring to Hawes. They did not really see beyond cotton spinning, but in its long life since, the mill has harnessed water power for a bewildering range of functions, flax spinning, wool spinning, woodworking machinery and electricity generation for the village. In 1988 the mill finally closed its doors as a commercial operation, and the building fell into disrepair.

"The mill has harnessed water power for a bewildering range of functions, flax spinning, wool spinning, woodworking machinery and electricity generation for the village."

That could have been it had it not been for local volunteers who joined the Gayle Mill Trust and worked tirelessly to return the mill to its former glory. One of the team, Tony Routh, was its last apprentice back in the 1960s. 'It was like coming home,' he said. 'When we started the project, the building was just as it was the day that I walked out and into a new job – a few more cobwebs perhaps, and a bit more lime off the walls. We've come a long way since then though, and it's great to see it now, completely brought back to life.'

Coming third in the national final of the BBC's *Restoration* series in 2004 proved crucial in securing funds and now the turbines are turning again to produce electricity and work timber once more. The mill is open for tours, and a shop sells hand-crafted wood products made on site. If you want to get involved, sign up for one of their two-day working courses.

Gayle has two other aquatic attractions. **Blackburn Farm** (01969 667524) has a small lake stocked with rainbow trout available for angling, and a footpath to stroll alongside Gayle Beck upstream. A lovely walk in itself, but it has the added bonus of **Aysgill Force** waterfall, about a mile away and especially impressive at high water levels.

3 HARDRAW

Green Dragon Inn (see page 176)

This sleepy little hamlet follows a typical Dales formula: an old pub, a new church on an old site, a stone bridge over a small beck and a scattering of other buildings, some farms and some cottages, with one tea room-cum-craft shop. What makes Hardraw different is that on land just upstream of the Green Dragon Inn, belonging to it as part of its back garden (so you have to pass through the pub and pay an entrance fee), the beck leaps off an overhanging 100-foot limestone cliff. This is **Hardraw Force**, the highest clear fall waterfall above ground in England. The whole place has a steady, timeless air about it – a feeling of permanence – but appearances can be deceptive.

"The whole place has a steady, timeless air about it – a feeling of permanence – but appearances can be deceptive."

Hardraw very nearly didn't exist at all beyond 1889. Hardraw Beck is only a small stream, in fact in mid-summer it is not usually much more than a trickle, and on the morning of 12 July that is just how things were. By the afternoon though, things were very different and at the end of the day known ever since as the Great Flood, Hardraw was all but wiped off the map. Around noon livid black clouds over Shunner Fell burst into ferocious rain with the deafening crack of thunder. Thousands of tons of water roared down the hillside and funnelled into Hardraw Beck. By the time it reached the village terrified residents watched a wall of water yards high tear around the corner and slam into buildings;

all were flooded and some demolished. The graveyard was torn up and coffins and gravestones washed two miles downstream. A huge tree smashed a hole in the wall of the Green Dragon Inn and all the bridges disappeared completely.

Dales folk are resilient and Hardraw was repaired and rebuilt, but one reconstruction not many people are aware of is the waterfall itself. Such was the power of the surge that the lip of the falls was scoured away and Hardraw Force became a cascade down rock and loose boulders, losing its title of highest clear fall in the process. The landowner at the time, Lord Wharncliffe, wasn't having that. On inspecting the damage, he turned to his estate manager and commanded, 'Put it all back.' The very best stonemasons were hired and the lip was rebuilt to its previous shape. Few of today's thousands of visitors to Hardraw Force realise that they are looking at a manmade top to the cliff, still cunningly secured with metal pins.

"The acoustics of the gorge here are perfect for outdoor music apparently, so once a year in early September it is the venue for a prestigious brass band competition."

Not all people visit Hardraw Scar to view the waterfall; the acoustics of the gorge here are perfect for outdoor music apparently, so once a year in early September it is the venue for a prestigious brass band competition.

If Hardraw Force has whetted your appetite for waterfalls, then you will really enjoy Fossdale's neighbouring valley. Cotterdale wraps around the western flank of Great Shunner Fell and is drained by two beautiful becks, East and West Gill, which between them boast nine waterfalls. They join forces to form Cotterdale Beck and produce three more cascades, the final one, **Cotter Force**, being the most impressive. It is also the most accessible, on foot or by wheelchair, 300 yards from the A684 at Holme Heads Bridge.

¶¶ FOOD & DRINK

The Cart House Hardraw ✆ 01969 667691. A bridge-side café offering homemade, and mostly organic, food, and with a craft shop attached.

Green Dragon Inn Hardraw ✆ 01969 667392 ⌂ www.greendragonhardraw.com. Worth a recommendation for the 13th-century building and well-kept selection of beers alone. This must be the only pub in the country with its own waterfall; access to Hardraw Force is via here for a fee. A wide variety of accommodation is available (see page 176).

MID WENSLEYDALE: ASKRIGG TO WEST WITTON

4 ASKRIGG

It is a sad indictment of our society's priorities, I think, that Askrigg should be most famous as a film set for a television series rather than as a village of great character and rich history. But, it's **James Herriot** country we are in, and this is the fictional village of Darrowby from *All Creatures Great and Small*, the series about a Yorkshire vet.

Askrigg is very old, with evidence of Iron Age settlement, but the name is younger and pure Norse, describing its position admirably on a ridge of high ground (rigg) where ash trees (ask) grow. The village's heyday was in the 1700s when it had the only market in Upper Wensleydale, a booming textile industry (hand knitting mainly) and a reputation for clock-making. The local lords of the manor were the Metcalfes who ruled the roost from nearby Nappa Hall, once an impressive 15th-century fortified manor house but now a working farm and a little decrepit. One of many fine short walks from Askrigg takes in the hall and Nappa Mill before returning to the village via the banks of the River Ure.

> *"Askrigg is very old but the name is younger and pure Norse, describing its position admirably on a ridge of high ground (rigg) where ash trees (ask) grow."*

Askrigg's market ceased trading long ago when Hawes took over as the local commercial centre, but the **market cross** is still here, as is a reminder of a cruel past. An iron ring is still set into the market place cobbles, where bulls would be tied, to be baited with dogs. The **bull-ring** was also used for another purpose, a sort of heavy gauntlet-throwing challenge, where a man wanting a fight would turn the ring over and another fancying his chances would turn it back. Presumably they would then set to knocking lumps off one another.

Most of Askrigg's interesting old buildings are clustered around or near the marketplace. St Oswald's Church is here, as is the Kings Arms (TV's very own Drovers Arms in the Herriot series) with Skeldale House Vet's Surgery in nearby Cringley Lane – its real name is Cringley House. None of the village textile mills are still in operation but one, Low Mill, is very active in another way, as an outdoor activities centre.

A handy waterside **walk** from the village traces the upstream course of the beck that used to power Low Mill's wheel. Your rewards for following Mill Gill are views of a series of pretty waterfalls wrapped in folds of oak woodland, culminating after a mile or so in the highest, **Whitfield Gill Force**. At this point you can return to Askrigg via an old green lane or carry on uphill to explore the scars, shake holes and swallow holes of Whitfield Fell.

¶¶ FOOD & DRINK

Askrigg Village Kitchen Market Pl ✆ 01969 650076 ⌂ www.askriggvillagekitchen.co.uk. One of those does-everything places. The only tea shop in the village but also a deli, bakery, shop and post office.

Crown Inn Main St ✆ 01969 650298. Locals refer to this as the 'Top Pub', the Kings Arms being the 'Bottom Pub', and this is their preferred drinking place. Beer is Black Sheep and Theakstons; traditional pub grub.

Kings Arms Main St ✆ 01969 650817. This is the Drovers Arms of *All Creatures Great and Small* fame as celebrity photos on the walls testify. It was chosen because it looked so traditional-old-Yorkshire and it still does. What's more, the welcome is genuinely friendly: Theakstons, Black Sheep and house beer brewed by Askrigg's own brewery.

ACTIVITIES

Low Mill Station Rd ✆ 01969 650432 ⌂ www.lowmill.com. A residential outdoor centre with a wide range of activities: canoeing, climbing, caving and the like, for groups. They cater mainly for school groups, but if you are staying locally you can pre-hire an instructor for up to ten of you for a day's activity of your choice.

5 BAINBRIDGE

🏠 **Gill Edge Cottages** (see page 176)

Bainbridge is a mere mile from Askrigg as the curlew flies, but a meandering two via the road over Yore Bridge. It is a similar size to its neighbour and probably at least as old; a Bronze Age earthwork sits just to the south, and on top of Brough Hill a Roman fort. The Latin invaders named this place Virosidum. Modern-day Bainbridge is a strangely sprawling settlement which suffers more than a little from having a busy 'A' road cut across the village green.

The village does have one famous old tradition which, after a sad lapse, has recently started again: that of the blowing of the Forest Horn. Back in the 14th century when much of Upper Wensleydale was hunting forest, a horn was sounded every winter night at 22.00 to guide benighted travellers in the forest safely back to Bainbridge. This custom was continued for hundreds of years but was only documented in the 19th century when the role of horn-blower was passed down the Metcalfe family. An old cow horn dating back to 1611 was replaced in 1864 with the present one, a huge African buffalo horn that resides in the Rose and Crown Hotel. Starting on 27 September, which is the feast of the Holy Rood for those that don't know, a long, clear blast of the horn echoes around the dale each evening, and continues to brighten the winter nights until Shrovetide the following February.

"The village does have one famous old tradition which, after a sad lapse, has recently started again: that of the blowing of the Forest Horn."

¶¶ FOOD & DRINK

Corn Mill Tea Room Newkin DL8 3EH ☎ 01969 650212. Within earshot of the River Bain. Lunches, afternoon tea and snacks. Lemon meringue pie to die for. Open Easter–Oct.

Schoolhouse Farm Stalling Busk DL8 3DH ☎ 01969 650233 ⏱ www.raydalepreserves. co.uk. A small tea shop and mini-museum on a farm that produces its own Raydale Preserves. Have a cuppa and a slice of homemade cake and then take away a jar of jam or chutney for later. Open May–Oct.

6 SEMER WATER

Natural lakes are in short supply in Yorkshire so consequently the few that exist tend to earn undeserved fame. Semer Water, in little Raydale, is trumpeted as the largest lake in North Yorkshire but at less than half a mile long it is not going to excite anyone who has visited the Lake District. It is also supposed to conceal a drowned town under its surface, but with a maximum depth of 30 feet it could scarcely hide a solitary two-storey building. Having said all that, Semer Water is a gorgeous place, a haven for winter wildfowl and summer watersports with a rich enough mix of marshland wildlife to prompt the Yorkshire Wildlife Trust to declare it a nature reserve.

The legend of the flooded town, while patently not true, is an entertaining moral homily. The gist of the story is that a wandering saint visited bustling Semer Town disguised as a pauper and begging food and shelter. He was rudely turned away from every house save that of a poor, old couple who treated him like one of the family. The following day he cursed the town with the words:

Semer Water rise! Semer Town sink!
And bury the place all save the house
Where they gave me meat and drink.

You can park at the north end of the lake for a small fee in summer, but for peace and quiet head down to the other end. Here, the wetland nature reserve is a glorious place to explore in early summer with the spongy ground festooned with water-loving plants, nothing very rare, but a wide variety including marsh valerian, bog bean, ragged robin, marsh cinquefoil and marsh and spotted orchids, with yellow water-lilies on the open water. Crooks Beck wriggles its way through the marsh to empty into Semer Water, but when it emerges at the other end of the lake it is now known as the River Bain. Its 1½-mile journey to the River Ure makes it the shortest river in England, but in that brief distance it does manage to boast a population of native crayfish and some of the finest brown trout fishing in the Dales.

7 AYSGARTH

✦ Temple Folly Swinithwaite (see page 176)

This is an odd split-site village with the main settlement, presumably the original 'clearing in the oaks', half a mile away from the most visited buildings clustered around the famous Aysgarth Falls. **St Andrew's Church** is here, on the hillside overlooking Yore Mill and the river. The church is the probable original reason for the separation; it is a restored 16th-century building but almost certainly on an older religious site, maybe even pagan, connected with the Falls. It was at its most influential during medieval times when the church was owned by Jervaulx Abbey (see page 132). Its present claims to fame are the old abbey rood screen and vicar's stall that were moved here at the time of the Dissolution. This work of art was too valuable to dismantle so was carried the 13 miles in one piece on the shoulders of 20 men.

"Its present claims to fame are the old abbey rood screen and vicar's stall that were moved here at the time of the Dissolution."

It is the River Ure that most people come here to see, or more specifically, its 200-foot descent in the space of less than half a mile that constitutes the **Aysgarth Falls**. There is no single spectacular drop but a series of limestone terraced steps at High Force, Middle Force, Lower Force and a further unnamed waterfall lower down – let's call it Bottom Force. Come here after a dry spell and you will wonder what all the fuss is about but if the river is full the name 'force' becomes more meaningful and the roar of the combined drops can be heard a long way away.

However big and brown the Ure is, the **riverside walking** is a delight, and accessible for wheelchairs and pushchairs all the way to Middle Force. The only drawback for me is the crowds; it can get very busy with the adjacent national park visitor centre attracting its quota of visitors. It's not too difficult to find a little solitude though, as most people stroll to the falls and back on the north bank. If you walk through the churchyard and down to the river on the other side you may well find that you have it to yourself. Alternatively, head away from the river into Freeholders' Wood where the National Park has reinstated a traditional hazel-coppicing system and is currently encouraging the return of the common dormouse to its preferred habitat. Look out for their nest boxes in the shrubbery.

"The National Park has reinstated a hazel-coppicing system encouraging the return of the common dormouse to its natural habitat."

Beyond the woods, a choice of **footpaths** can take you to the villages north of Aysgarth and the river: Carperby with its fine pub, the Wheatsheaf, and old market cross; Redmire, the present terminus of the Wensleydale Railway; and Castle Bolton. South of the river the main valley is joined by the tributary Bishopdale and, slightly removed downstream, the village of West Witton.

Close to the falls, **Yore Mill** is an imposing four-storey building built in 1784, the same year as Gayle Mill (see page 114). It is not quite so precious to industrial archaeologists, as it was substantially rebuilt in 1852 after a fire, but it still merits Grade 2 listed status. It has changed jobs through its long life, cotton spinning first, then knitting yarn and later corn grinding and flour rolling. For ten years after milling finished in the 1950s Yore Mill was a cattle food depot and until recently a horse-drawn carriage museum. At present it just houses a tea shop and self-catering flat for two, but the owners have plans to restore the building, wheel and turbines to generate power again. Let's hope they manage it.

¶¶ FOOD & DRINK

Berry's Farm Shop Swinithwaite DL8 4UH ☎ 01969 663377 ⌂ http://berrysfarmshop.
com. A farm shop, café and lots besides run by the owner occupiers of Swinithwaite Hall in
their farm courtyard. They pride themselves on excellent sustainable credentials throughout.
George and Dragon Inn Main St, Aysgarth DL8 3AD ☎ 01969 663358 ⌂ www.
georgeanddragonaysgarth.co.uk. A Grade 2 listed 17th-century coaching inn with separate
bar and restaurant. Excellent food is a mixture of traditional local and fine cuisine. Beer is
all brewed in Wensleydale (Black Sheep and Yorkshire Dales beers) and the wine selection is
extensive. Can get packed; open all day.
Hamiltons Tea Rooms Aysgarth DA8 3AE ☎ 01969 663423 ⌂ www.yoredalehouse.com.
Very welcoming and comfortable. Part of Yoredale House B&B. Open Wed-Sun.
Mill Race Teashop Aysgarth Falls DL8 3SR ☎ 01969 663446 ⌂ www.themillraceteashop.
co.uk. Great views of Upper Falls. Twenty different teas, outrageous hedonistic hot chocolate,
real coffee and homemade cakes and scones. Also sells local produce.

8 CASTLE BOLTON & REDMIRE

'My name is Sir Richard le Scrope and I have a licence to crenellate,'
sounds like a line John Cleese could have uttered in *Monty Python and
the Holy Grail*, but truth can be stranger than fiction. Sir Richard was
the builder in 1379 and like all 14th-century
castle-builders, he needed a licence to put
turrets on his towers.

*"Bolton Castle is
a particularly
rewarding place to
visit, partly because
it is so complete,
but also because it
is privately owned
so hasn't had the
corporate treatment."*

Bolton Castle (DL8 4ET ☎ 01969 623981
⌂ www.boltoncastle.co.uk) is a particularly
rewarding place to visit, partly because it is
so complete, but also because it is privately
owned so hasn't had the corporate treatment
some historic buildings suffer. The owner has
considerable emotional investment in the place
because, incredibly, the castle has remained in
one family throughout its entire 600-year history. Harry Orde-Powlett,
the present eighth Lord Bolton, is a direct descendant of Sir Richard the
Crenellator. Incidentally, the building is Bolton Castle and the village it's
in is Castle Bolton.

There is so little damage to the fabric of the building because the
Royalist defenders surrendered after six months of passive siege in the
Civil War, during another Pythonesque episode in the castle's history.
Colonel Chaytor, the commander of the Royalists, apparently cut off his

own hand and threw it at his enemies in an extreme gesture of defiance but, not surprisingly, this didn't work and the siege continued, with the defenders finally giving up after eating their last horse. The Scropes regained the castle after Cromwell's demise but moved out to the newly constructed luxury mansion of Bolton Hall near Wensley and the castle became a block of flats of sorts with up to nine families living in it up until the 1940s.

"Special events are held throughout the year, such as armada or medieval weekends, which involve a lot of dressing up."

Now uninhabited, the castle has been developed as an excellent visitor attraction (open April to October), with the bulk of it restored and accessible. Much is made of Castle Bolton's most illustrious past resident, Mary, Queen of Scots, who spent an eventful six months here in 1568 after her capture by Queen Elizabeth's forces in Scotland. She was ostensibly imprisoned, but local Catholic sympathisers made her stay very comfortable, supplying cartloads of tapestries, Turkish carpets, luxury clothes and venison – certainly not the conditions that the wretches in the dungeons had to suffer.

The gardens have been relaid along medieval lines including a herb garden, maze, bowling green, rose garden and what must be one of the most northerly vineyards in the country. Regular special events are held throughout the year, such as armada or medieval weekends, which involve lots of dressing up and period activities – the kids will probably love them, and you can leave them to it while you visit the gift shop and tea room.

A choice of two roads or two footpaths will take you downhill from Castle Bolton to its near neighbour, **Redmire**. What brings most people here is the **Wensleydale Railway** (see below), this being the present terminus of the line. If you have arrived by rail, and have time to kill before your train back, a three-mile circular walk taking in the ancient sunken track of Thoresby Lane and Castle Bolton is an excellent way to do it.

The Wensleydale Railway

Runs throughout the year, Redmire to Leeming Bar (journey time 50 minutes); see ⌂ www.boltonarmsredmire.co.uk for schedule.

'I have a dream,' one famous speech began, and so do the volunteers of the Wensleydale Railway Association (WRA). Their aim is to restore the rail link along the full 40-mile length of their beloved valley, from the East Coast Main Line at Northallerton, to the Settle–Carlisle line at Garsdale. This is not just a nostalgia trip by a group of middle-aged beardy types, or a cynical money-making tourist trap, but a genuine attempt to return the service that the local Dales people felt should never have been taken away. 'We'd love our railway to become the branch line it was in the 1920s and 30s,' said David Walker, one of the WRA volunteers, 'A thread linking all the communities of the dale from schoolchildren and commuters to tourists coming to visit this lovely part of the world.'

At present, 17 miles of operating line is marooned in the middle, between Leeming Bar and Redmire. Joining up the eastern end should be the easiest task, as it's only five miles to Northallerton, and the track is still in place and used for freight transport – the MOD bringing tanks to Catterick Garrison in the main. The major long-term project will be the relaying of 18 miles of track from Redmire, the present terminus, to Garsdale Head. This would mean the re-opening of stations in Askrigg and Hawes eventually, but the first goal is the next stop along the line after Redmire–Aysgarth.

'It's definitely a labour of love,' said David. 'None of us would put this amount of hard work in for free if we didn't enjoy it. It takes my head away from the day job and I've made a lot of new friends from all sorts of backgrounds – and contrary to popular perception, none of them are oddball eccentrics!'

¶¶ FOOD & DRINK

Bolton Arms Redmire DL8 4EA ✆ 01969 624336 ⌂ www.boltonarmsredmire.co.uk. A great all-round village pub very popular for evening meals. B&B available.
Bolton Castle Tea Room Castle Bolton DL8 4ET ✆ 01969 625617. Run by an ex-London chef, and not your average tea room.

9 BISHOPDALE

Few people are aware of Bishopdale, and even of those that are, not many stop and enjoy its delights. They are usually on their way from Wensleydale to Wharfedale, or vice-versa, on the 'B' road that runs its length. The upper dale is almost-deserted sheep and walking country with a scattering of farms, but lower down there are three villages, each with a pub. For **Newbiggin** that's just about it, **Thoralby** also has a chapel, post office and waterfall and **West Burton** is a veritable metropolis with all of the above plus school, village hall, general store, butchers and craft shops. It also boasts one of the largest and most oddly shaped market crosses in the country, a strange stretched pyramid of a thing on the extremely spacious village green. What originally brought me to West Burton though, was the same feature that attracted the landscape painter J M W Turner in the 19th century. Yards from the village centre, but hidden away in its own limestone amphitheatre, is **Cauldron Falls**, a beautiful cascade formed by Walden Beck's leap over a 15-foot rock step. Good swimming can be enjoyed in the pool below when it's warm and quiet enough. A short stroll of a mile or so follows Walden Beck upstream from the waterfall to Cote Bridge, then back over fields or road to the village.

FOOD & DRINK

Fox and Hounds Inn West Burton DL8 4JY ✆ 01969 663111 🖱 www.fhinn.co.uk. A 17th-century building on the village green with quoits pitch adjoining. It is the social centre of the village with something going on most evenings, including darts and dominoes teams. Cask beers, John Smith's and Theakstons, with other local guest beers.

10 WEST WITTON

🏠 **The Blue Lion** (see page 176)

If you have seen the film *The Wicker Man* then the goings-on here one Sunday, every August will send familiar shivers down your spine. The name 'West Witton' is so innocent-sounding, and the local people are very decent really, but on St Bartholomew's Day every year they all take part in a ritual of barbaric pagan origins. It's called the Burning of Bartle and re-enacts supposed real historical events when a local criminal is chased, caught and burned at the stake in place of a sacrificial lamb. The route of the chase is recounted in a chanted verse:

On Penhill crags he tore his rags
At Hunters Thorn he blew his horn
At Capplebank Stee he brak his knee
At Grassgill Beck he brak his neck
At Wadhams End he couldn't fend
At Grassgill End we'll mak his end
SHOUT LADS SHOUT!

To the accompaniment of a rousing cheer from the crowd, a straw effigy is set alight and everyone marches, singing, to the pub for a pint or two – it's very sinister stuff. This traditional ceremony has been carried out for at least 400 years and the villagers are very proud of it, so much so that the local youth club, with help from Rural Arts, North Yorkshire, produced a series of mosaic tiles telling the story. They are in place up on the hillside making up a trail which you can follow during a pleasant four-mile fell walk.

¶| FOOD & DRINK

Fox and Hounds Main St 📞 01969 623630 🖰 www.foxwitton.com. A characterful 13th-century building housing a classic beer-drinkers' local.
Wensleydale Heifer Main St 📞 01969 622322 🖰 www.wensleydaleheifer.co.uk. I nearly didn't get past the tacky pub sign, and what a mistake that would have been. This is a fantastic fish restaurant in a pub, miles from the sea, not cheap but top quality. Black Sheep beer available.

LOWER WENSLEYDALE: WENSLEY TO BEDALE

11 WENSLEY

In 1956 schoolchildren made a strange discovery in Holy Trinity churchyard, a seemingly deliberately buried market cross. This odd ritual of laying to rest the symbol of a town's identity encapsulates Wensley's sad history and explains why Wensleydale is named after such a tiny village. In the 14th and 15th centuries this was the market town for the whole of the dale, but in 1563 the plague struck and Wensley was particularly badly hit. Most inhabitants died, others moved to nearby Leyburn and certainly no-one had any intention of visiting the market. There was probably nothing to sell anyway, the parish crop register noting grimly, 'This year nothing set down.' Wensley has never fully recovered its former importance and, but for Lord Bolton building his hall nearby, might have faded away completely. Today however it is one of the most appealing of the dale's villages, and well worth a visit.

The old church is still there, along with the village pub and a Victorian watermill which now houses a traditional candle maker. **White Rose Candle Workshop** (📞 01969 623544 🖰 www.whiterosecandles.co.uk)

A Ure-side stroll

❈ OS Explorer map OL30; start: Wensley bridge, grid reference SE091894.

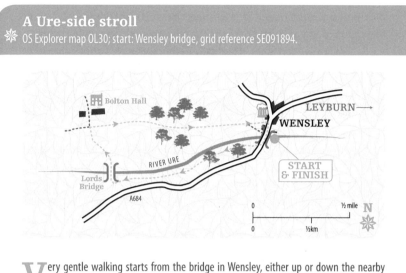

Very gentle walking starts from the bridge in Wensley, either up or down the nearby River Ure. If you head upstream (westwards) for a mile along the south bank and over Lords Bridge you can return via Bolton Hall, which isn't open to the public but a public footpath passes right in front of the hall – I'm sure Lord Bolton loves that!

has been the White family business since 1978, producing traditional beeswax and other candles of all shapes, sizes, designs and scents. It is a fascinating experience, and one that I found strangely relaxing, to watch the candles being made. Admission is free and you can also enjoy the small waterfall by the side of the mill. The workshop is open on various Fridays, Saturdays and Sundays throughout the year – check before you go.

🍴 FOOD & DRINK

The Three Horseshoes Wensley DL8 4HJ ☎ 01969 622327. This cosy village inn is a beer drinkers' pub with a good changing range of well-kept Yorkshire cask ales. Open every evening and most lunchtimes.

12 LEYBURN

This pleasant and, seemingly, always busy market town is easily the largest settlement in this part of Lower Wensleydale though it has limited attractions of its own. I like Leyburn but I must admit I can't be entertained for very long within the town itself. It desperately tries to borrow a bit of history from Bolton Castle in its Leyburn Shawl story, where Mary, Queen of Scots was said to have escaped from Bolton Castle but dropped her shawl on the cliffs above Leyburn, thus betraying her whereabouts and causing her recapture. Wishful balderdash I'm afraid; Leyburn Shawl Crag's name is much older than the Tudors and has its root in the word 'shielings' or shepherds' huts. Retracing the queen's supposed footsteps back along the Shawl top to the castle makes a splendid walk though, with glorious panoramic views.

"Mary, Queen of Scots was said to have dropped her shawl on the cliffs of Leyburn, thus betraying her whereabouts and causing her recapture."

No, Leyburn is not an historical centre but it is an effective service centre for the dale with the wide variety of shops, a market every Friday and a farmers' market every fourth Saturday of the month. It also has one of the largest **antiques auction rooms** in the country in the form of Tennants (Harmby Rd ☎ 01969 623780 ⏱ www.tennants.co.uk). The town hosts two big annual events: the **Wensleydale Show** on August Bank Holiday Saturday and the **Dales Festival of Food and Drink** on May Day weekend are both a real treat.

Just downstream of Leyburn and Middleham, the River Ure is joined by the River Cover, the latter having just navigated the length of Coverdale, another little valley on a par with Bishopdale for unspoiled pastoral peace.

¶¶ FOOD & DRINK

Penley's Coffee Shop Market Pl ☎ 01969 623909. Particularly good cappuccino and some very tasty and good-value snacks. Open in daytime, plus evenings Fri and Sat.

Rupali Balti House High St ☎ 01969 624863. Deserves a mention as one of the best take-away curry houses I have encountered anywhere in Yorkshire.

Sandpiper Inn Railway St ☎ 01969 622206 ⏱ www.sandpiperinn.co.uk. One of Leyburn's oldest buildings is home to its best food, courtesy of host/chef Jonathan Harrison. Menus are based on local farm produce and game, expertly prepared and reasonably priced. Not especially a drinkers' pub unless your tipple is malt whisky with over 100 to choose from. Closed Mon.

Serendipity Tearooms High St ☎ 01969 625388. A different sort of place on the first floor over a crafty gift shop. Open daily.

13 MIDDLEHAM

Two miles south of Leyburn and perched on high land between the rivers Ure and Cover, sits the village of Middleham. It has three links with royalty: the childhood home of a king, royal treasure and the sport of kings. The impressive remains on the edge of the village are, in fact, Middleham Castle mark two, its predecessor still visible as a mound on William's Hill just south and up the slope. Richard III was brought up here as a lad in the 15th century under the tutelage of the Earl of Warwick.

"The impressive remains on the edge of the village are, in fact, Middleham Castle mark two, its predecessor still visible as a mound on William's Hill."

It was then that he met the Earl's daughter Anne, whom he later married, thus inheriting the castle on Warwick's death. He became king on the death of his brother Edward IV in 1483 but his reign was a short and miserable one. Within the space of two years his only son died in the castle aged 11, his wife went the same way the following year aged 28, and he also supposedly uttered those famous words, 'A horse, a horse, my kingdom for a horse,' at the Battle of Bosworth. He didn't get his horse and lost the battle, his kingdom and his life aged 31. We have Shakespeare to thank for the quote and the all-round impression of a vindictive, malicious and selfish character. Modern historians are of the view that the Bard was trying to impress the reigning Tudors with his writing and that Richard was quite a nice chap on the whole. The villagers would certainly agree; their local king is still remembered with much affection and a requiem mass is said in the village church annually on 22 August, the anniversary of his death.

THE MIDDLEHAM JEWEL

A right royal treasure was found near Middleham Castle in 1985 by Ted Seaton, an amateur metal detector. He was about to pack up and go home when his machine picked up a faint signal from just over a foot beneath the soil surface. Ted dug out what he thought was an old compact box and took it home to clean. It was then he discovered what he had; a diamond-shaped gold pendant inlaid with a single sapphire and exquisitely engraved with a scene of the Trinity and a Latin charm against 'falling sickness' (epilepsy). The Middleham Jewel, as it has come to be known, was bought by the Yorkshire Museum in York for the tidy sum of £2.5 million.

An almost perfectly straight two-mile stretch of bridleway leads from Middleham over Low Moor to the west, and on the map it looks like a deserted trackway ideal for a peaceful walk or bike ride. If you do venture up, solitude you won't find but entertainment you will, as on most days, scores of racehorses thunder up and down it on their way to or from the old racecourse on High Moor. There hasn't been an official race here since 1873 but the training tradition, once started, continued. Today no fewer than 15 stables operate in and around Middleham, making it one of the biggest horse-racing centres in the country. If you want to see more than just the horses around the lanes and on the gallops, then pay a small fee and book on a morning stable tour (℡ 07857 379880 or 07857 379878 ⌖ www.middlehamracingtours.co.uk).

⏍ FOOD & DRINK

There is decent food and drink on hand in Middleham, but if you want better than just decent it's worth travelling a couple of miles out of town to one of these:

The Blue Lion East Witton DL8 4SN ℡ 01969 624273 ⌖ www.thebluelion.co.uk. Between Middleham and Jervaulx Abbey on the A6108, this old coaching inn is an almost perfect blend of flag-floored, open-fired village pub bar and country house hotel. While the beer is fine, Black Sheep and other local cask ales, the emphasis is on the food which is wholesome traditional fare of fantastic quality. Not cheap but worth it.

Cover Bridge Inn East Witton DL8 4SQ ℡ 01969 623250 ⌖ www.thecoverbridgeinn.co.uk. Another old coaching inn, this is in a glorious location at the confluence of the rivers Ure and Cover. Riverside walks from the door and fishing permits from behind the bar.

14 COVERDALE

Medieval monks and nuns sought out beautiful and isolated places for their abbeys and priories so it's no surprise that ecclesiastical remains are scattered around Coverham and East Scrafton in this valley. Middleham Church is dedicated to the nun St Alkelda (see page 56); perhaps she was a resident of the abbey in Coverdale. Little documentary evidence has been found concerning the Premonstratensian order (Ordo Praemonstratensis) that lived here – I suspect because few people could either spell or pronounce the name. Coverdale is still relatively isolated and definitely beautiful, a hidden corner some may call it, which is apt because its most popular attraction is the **Forbidden Corner**, a fantasy-based series of mazes and follies in the four-acre garden of an old racing horse stables, Tupgill Park.

The Forbidden Corner

Tupgill Park Estate, Coverham DL8 4TJ ☎ 01969 640638 ✆ www.theforbiddencorner.co.uk;
Open Apr–Oct daily and Nov–Christmas Sun only; under 4s free; tickets must be booked in
advance online or by phone, or bought on the day from Leyburn Tourist Information Centre
if there are any left.

This place in Coverdale, west of Middleham, quite justifiably advertises
itself as 'The Strangest Place in the World'. It is brilliantly unique and
although it was voted top family day out in a national survey, beating
Alton Towers and Legoland, it was never
intended as anything more than a private
family folly. It was the brainchild of the owner
of Tupgill Park, Colin Armstrong, who in
the 1980s teamed up with architect Malcolm
Tempest to design a series of walled gardens,
tunnels, grottoes and towers which linked into
a three-dimensional maze for his family and friends to explore. As it
developed it was opened to the public and its fame spread by word of
mouth, to the point now where it can barely cope with its own popularity.

"The entrance through the gaping mouth of a giant stone monster sets the tone and away you go."

What makes it so good is that it is a genuine adventure. On arrival you
are given a leaflet which is not a map, but a series of cryptic messages.
'All the clues to finding your way around are on the sheet,' a girl at the
reception said. 'They're just not in the right order.' The entrance through
the gaping mouth of a giant stone monster sets the tone and away you
go. I first came here in the early days when my children were small and
they absolutely loved it. We spent hours climbing, crawling, getting
lost, studying clues, groping along dark corridors, planning routes
from battlement viewpoints, getting lost again and finally finding the
way to the underground temple. At times I was genuinely unnerved,
for example by the revolving room with identical doors, and after two
subsequent visits, some secret corners have still managed to evade me.

This is a must-see place, especially if you have children, but I would
strongly recommend coming at less busy times to make the most of the
sense of exploration.

15 CONSTABLE BURTON

You'll find this village three miles east of Leyburn on the Bedale road.
If you have been looking for it you might have been intending to
visit the Wyvill Arms pub for some of its very good food, or the

Wyvill family home at **Constable Burton Hall** (✆ 01677 450428 ⁿ www.constableburtongardens.com; gardens open mid Mar–Sep; guided tours by arrangement). If you end up near Hull in East Yorkshire, your satnav has taken you to Burton Constable not Constable Burton – an easy mistake, and you're not the first. The hall is a Grade 1 listed neo classical Georgian mansion set in a large landscaped park. It is the park and gardens that most people come to visit, partly because they are attractive, and well worth the entrance fee, but mainly because the hall is not usually open to the public.

16 JERVAULX ABBEY

This abbey suffered more than most under Henry VIII's violent Dissolution and sadly, very little of it remains. It was a very influential daughter house of the Cistercian Byland Abbey with the original French monks probably responsible for starting cheese making in Wensleydale. What remains today are peaceful and atmospheric ruins which the private owners have allowed to become overgrown by 180 species of wild plants – a lovely floral oasis. Entrance is every day of the year by honesty-box payment. The tea rooms and gift shop on the opposite side of the road are open mid-March to October.

Brymor Ice Cream

High Jervaulx Farm, HG4 4PG ✆ 01677 460337 ⁿ www.abmoore.co.uk.

At High Jervaulx Farm, above the abbey, the Cistercian monks' dairy-produce tradition continues; not cheese nowadays but ice cream. Brymor Ice Cream is available throughout Yorkshire in 30 flavours but what makes it so popular is its rich creaminess – how do they do it? The answer is pedigree Guernsey cows and lush Dales pasture. Brymor is one of the few on-farm producers of ice cream that only uses milk from the farm's own herd so they can guarantee the provenance of the product, and its richness – Guernsey cow milk has one of the highest fat contents of any available. There are three ways you can sample the delights of

"Brymor is one of the few on-farm producers of ice cream that only uses milk from the farm's own herd so they can guarantee the provenance of the product, and its richness."

rum and raisin, experiment with mocha almond crunch or remember nostalgic childhoods with traditional vanilla. You can look out for

Brymor Ice Cream served in cafés and restaurants in Yorkshire, you can buy it from good delis and farmers' markets or you can call in to High Jervaulx Farm and get it fresh. Either relax and eat it here in the conservatory or take it away along with some clotted cream and cheese if you wish.

17 BEDALE

Yet another town that dubs itself 'Gateway to the Dales', Bedale does have a justifiable claim as far as Wensleydale is concerned. If you enter the dale from the east, off the A1, or by train on the Wensleydale Railway, you will pass through this ancient market town.

Bedale is quite small and all the interest is concentrated on the long, thin marketplace, and the beck-side that runs parallel, so you can see just about everything on a half-mile stroll up one and down the other. The best place to start is Bedale Hall at the top of the market, opposite the church, where the town's small, free **Bedale Museum** (✆ 01677 427516 🖰 www.bedalemuseum.org.uk; open Apr–Sep) is a collection of bygones amassed over half a century and featuring an 18th-century wooden fire engine; from the adjacent tourist office you can pick up a heritage trail leaflet. I couldn't help but notice **St Gregory's Church** next door, and the disproportionate size of its tower. Apparently this most fortified church in the north of England was refuge for the townsfolk when the Scots came rampaging. Emgate leads from the 14th-century market cross down to the beck, which was part canalised in the 19th century to link Bedale with the River Swale, but abandoned when the railway arrived. The Harbour, a canal basin, is a reminder of these times gone, but nowhere near as impressive as the small square brick building on the far bank. This Grade 2 listed structure is unique; Britain's only remaining **leech house**, a store place for apothecaries' wriggly medical helpers.

"The Harbour, a canal basin, is a reminder of these times gone, but nowhere near as impressive as the small square brick building on the far bank."

Wandering back up the mainly Georgian, cobbled marketplace gives the opportunity for some browsing, especially on Tuesday's market day when the town's five pubs are at their atmospheric bustling best too. Of the four cafés, Aunt Sally's is probably the best.

On the eastern edge of Bedale, **Big Sheep Little Cow** (Aiskew Farm, DL8 1AW ☎ 01677 422125 🖰 www.farmattraction.co.uk) is a bit of a 'fast' children's attraction with an adventure play area and buggy rides, but its Slow credentials are earned with farm tours and home-produced dexter beef and ice cream for sale.

🍴 FOOD & DRINK

Cockburn's Butchers Market Pl ☎ 01677 422126 🖰 www.cockburnsbutchers.co.uk. A proper butchers, like they all used to be. Whenever I pass through Bedale I can't resist stopping here for a pie of some sort.

Farmhouse Bakery Market Pl ☎ 01677 424411. A traditional High Street bakery with a café attached. Lovely home-cooked food, as you would expect.

Pubs

Sadly, Bedale's pubs have seen better days but two in villages nearby are well worth the effort of getting to:

Buck Inn Village Green, Thornton Watlass HG4 4AH ☎ 01677 422461 🖰 www.buckwatlass. co.uk. Traditional village pub with cricket theme and field next door; beer from both Masham breweries plus micro-guests. Popular eating place with a good reputation locally. Dog-friendly B&B.

Castle Arms Inn Top of the Green, Snape DL8 2TB ☎ 01677 470270 🖰 www. castlearmsinn.com. A friendly, low-ceilinged, flagstoned village pub, just south of Thorp Perrow Arboretum. The menu is extensive, good value and top quality. Quiet annex B&B. Beer from Jennings and Marstons.

18 THORP PERROW ARBORETUM

DL8 2PS ☎ 01677 425323 🖰 www.thorpperrow.com; open all year.

What initially brought me to this place south of Bedale was joining a fungus foray event, to learn the useful skill of how not to poison myself eating wild mushrooms. In the process I was captivated by the autumn colours of the trees and shrubs planted by the arboretum's creator Sir Leonard Roper and also enjoyed a fascinating display of falconry at the bird centre. Other regular events that take place include photography courses, ghost walks, seasonal nature trails and outdoor concerts, and you can call in to the arboretum's tea room and gift shop without paying the entrance fee.

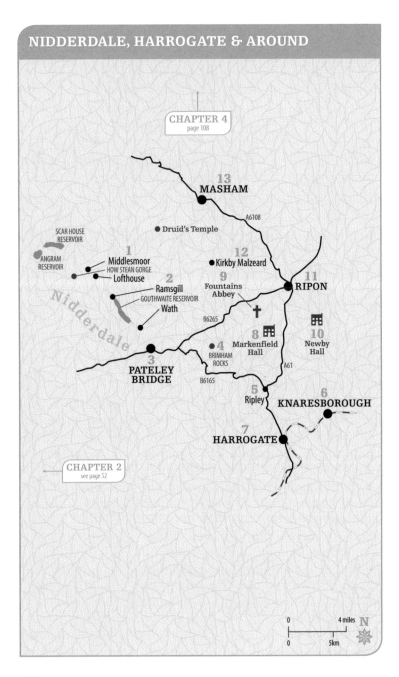

CHAPTER 4
page 108

13
MASHAM

A6108

SCAR HOUSE
RESERVOIR

● Druid's Temple

ANGRAM
RESERVOIR

1
Middlesmoor
HOW STEAN GORGE
Lofthouse

12
● Kirkby Malzeard

2
Ramsgill
GOUTHWAITE RESERVOIR
Wath

9
Fountains
Abbey

11
● **RIPON**

Nidderdale

B6265

8 Markenfield
Hall

10
Newby
Hall

4
BRIMHAM
ROCKS

A61

3
**PATELEY
BRIDGE**

B6165

5
Ripley

6
KNARESBOROUGH

7
HARROGATE

CHAPTER 2
see page 52

0   4 miles

0   5km

N

5
NIDDERDALE, HARROGATE & AROUND

Caroline Mills

Swaledale, Wensleydale or Wharfedale would, I'm sure, be the first to be mentioned if someone was asked to name one of the Yorkshire Dales in a pub quiz. But Nidderdale? It tends to play second or even third fiddle to the better-known dales. It isn't actually in the area designated as the Yorkshire Dales National Park at all. Hence the main throng of tourists tends to bypass Nidderdale, heading straight for the national park: in Nidderdale, the absence of visitors is almost tangible.

It is indeed strange that Nidderdale hasn't been included within the park boundary. The spectacular countryside around the dale is designated as an Area of Outstanding Natural Beauty. The hills that fall across the border between national park and AONB status are the same hills making up the same landscape.

Yet Nidderdale is a game of two halves. To the northwest, and closest to the Yorkshire Dales National Park, lies Upper Nidderdale. It's an area that becomes increasingly rugged and remote the further back along the valley you go. It pulls you like a magnet, drawing you further into its midst, tempting you with an ever-changing panorama at every turn, rise and fall. With only one small road that leads to nowhere, the hills of Little Whernside and its giant neighbour Great Whernside creating a wall between Nidderdale and Coverdale, there is no through traffic, unless you happen to be on foot or on horseback. A string of pearly reservoirs line the route of the River Nidd from the foot of its source, Great Whernside. These watering holes, quenching the thirst of residents in far-flung Bradford, are interspersed with tiny hamlets. The place is so remote

> *"Nidderdale pulls you like a magnet, drawing you further into its midst, tempting you with an ever-changing panorama at every turn, rise and fall."*

ℹ️ TOURIST INFORMATION

Harrogate Royal Baths, Crescent Rd ☎ 0845 389 3223
Knaresborough 9 Castle Courtyard ☎ 0845 389 0177
Masham Little Market Pl ☎ 01765 680200
Nidderdale AONB The Old Workhouse, Pateley Bridge ☎ 01423 712950
🖰 www.nidderdaleaonb.org.uk
Pateley Bridge 8 High St ☎ 0845 389 0179
Ripon Minster Rd ☎ 0845 389 0178

that a good guess would be required as to why anyone should have set up camp here years ago but now they have, it's easy to understand – for its quality of life that surpasses many others.

Further east, Nidderdale bottoms out, the hills recede and the land flattens. At least, the undulations are less undulating, the distance between villages decreases and the land becomes more cultivated. It's not until you reach **Knaresborough**, a good 30 miles from the river's source (and even longer if you stretched out the Nidd's meandering tendencies into a pencil-straight line), that you get any serious habitation although the elegant town of **Harrogate**, joined at the hip with Knaresborough on its eastern side, now sprawls further north and west towards the edge of Nidderdale AONB with a plethora of housing developments.

"Nidderdale bottoms out, the hills recede and the land flattens. At least, the undulations are less undulating."

Past Knaresborough, the Nidd continues for a few more meandering miles east before it disappears for good, its waters mingling with those of the more northerly Swale and Ure to form the mightier Ouse.

The Nidderdale AONB also swallows up the most southeasterly section of Wensleydale. Like its counterpart of Upper Nidderdale, the land furthest west begins harsh and inhospitable on top of Masham Moor before it drops down to greener pastures, great swathes of estate forests and a web of tiny tributaries that gurgle towards the Ure.

For this reason, Masham and Ripon, officially part of Wensleydale, are mentioned within this chapter but, for now, I'll stay with the upper reaches of Nidderdale before moving slowly southeast, just as the River Nidd does, towards Knaresborough and its neighbour, Harrogate.

SELF-POWERED TRAVEL

CYCLING

A free **bike-carrying service** is offered on the **Nidderdale Rambler** bus service from Harrogate and Pateley Bridge to Upper Nidderdale and Brimham Rocks although only three bikes per bus can be taken.

With so many lumps and bumps in the landscape, a few gears on the bike are necessary – even along the flatter stretches of the river valley. There's limited opportunity for **off-road cycling** around the cluster of villages and hamlets on the eastern side of the dale, with gentler slopes and quiet country lanes connecting them, making it easy to join the dots on the map. There are also a few extremely scenic, if arduous, bridleways high above on the moor. And there's always the odd pub or tea room to experience a bit of convivial communal spirit when you're thirsty.

In Harrogate and Knaresborough, there are lots of **cycle routes** to get around town. Harrogate Town Council has produced a network map for each town, which can be downloaded from their website (⌐ www.harrogate.gov.uk). The **Beryl Burton Cycle Way**, named after the seven-times world champion, connects Harrogate with Knaresborough along a 1½-mile stretch of traffic-free cycle path, avoiding the need to use the busy A59. One suspects the great Beryl might not have been that impressed, though – she was one of the toughest cyclists ever (of either sex) and, based on her 1973 record of 21 minutes 25 seconds for ten miles, it would have taken her less than four minutes to cover the distance!

A recent addition to this list of local cycle routes is an excellent four-miler called the **Nidderdale Greenway**. The re-opening of the old Nidd viaduct to walkers, bikes and horses has allowed access to the whole stretch of disused railway between Harrogate and Ripley.

Cycle hire is available from **How Stean Gorge** (✆ 01423 755666 ⌐ www.howstean.co.uk) in the heart of Upper Nidderdale, which caters to young families by hiring out child seats and tagalongs.

Secure covered **cycle parking** in Harrogate is available at both the Jubilee and Victoria car parks (next to the bus and railway station) and there are several bicycle shops in Harrogate. **Boneshakers Cycle Shop** (11 Albert St ✆ 01423 709453 ⌐ www.boneshakersbikes.co.uk) and **Spa Cycles** (1 Wedderburn Rd ✆ 01423 887003 ⌐ www.spacycles.co.uk) come highly recommended for repairs and servicing.

Group cycle rides around the Harrogate area

Formed in appreciation of a good cycle ride, **Wheel Easy!** (⊕ www.wheel-easy.org.uk) describe themselves on their website as 'Harrogate's cycling group for people who don't wear lycra! (and some who do)'. They cycle every Sunday and Wednesday morning throughout the year with the aim of appeasing everyone who likes to get on the saddle to enjoy the countryside – distances range from a 'short' ten-mile ride to medium (25 miles) and long-distance rides. Encouraging families to take part is crucial for the club but cyclists under the age of 18 must be accompanied by an adult and anyone under the age of 15 must be on a tandem cycle, in a child seat or on a trailer bike. There are specific all-age traffic-free bike rides planned throughout the year. All are welcome on their weekly rides – simply turn up at Hornbeam Park Railway Station (in Harrogate) at 09.30 on a Sunday (Wednesday morning times vary but usually begin at 09.30 or 10.00) with a roadworthy bike and a helmet.

Said Malcolm Margolis, one of the organisers of Wheel-Easy!, 'Our name describes exactly what we do; we are all about enjoying a leisurely cycle ride, not about racing so we really welcome anyone who is visiting the area to come on our rides with us and meet any number of our 200 members.' A list of rides is posted on the Wheel Easy! website should you favour a particular route but, whichever one you select, you'll find some great cycling in good company.

WALKING

Nidderdale has some great walking territory with spectacular views and scenery. There are opportunities for all, with many pre-planned short and medium-length routes across easy-going ground, which make good options for families. Wheelchair users can get out and about too at places like **Scar House**, where approximately two miles of the four-mile route around the reservoir is totally accessible. For walkers who like to stretch their legs, the **Nidderdale Way** trips its way over 53 miles of ground in a circular route that officially starts in Pateley Bridge. It provides the opportunity to walk around the uplands that nurture the juvenile River Nidd and along the riverbank to the greener pastures of lower-lying land further east. The route quite deliberately wiggles about a bit to take in some worthwhile landmarks such as Brimham Rocks and Ripley Castle but also links up with other footpaths and bridleways for circular day or half-day walks.

The **Dalesbus Ramblers** (⌂ www.dalesbusramblers.org.uk) organises a number of free, guided walks around the area that are all accessible by bus. Simply catch the bus to the starting point. Harrogate and Knaresborough have some rewarding **town walks** too, covered in this chapter; they can be particularly good for those with mobility issues, taking advantage of tarmac footpaths and pavements.

UPPER NIDDERDALE: NIDD HEAD TO PATELEY BRIDGE

It makes sense to begin at the beginning – where the River Nidd dribbles out from the fells around Great Whernside. Here the land is harsh and inhospitable, where the only sign of civilisation is the odd farmstead over the top of Great Whernside in Coverdale. Much of this land has open access rights so you can walk across the upland freely.

The first sign of human activity in Nidderdale is a couple of miles downstream where the river flows through two reservoirs, first **Angram** followed by **Scar House**. Angram is the older of the two, completed in 1919, while Scar House was the last of the Nidd reservoirs to be built, in 1936. The stone to build the giant dams was quarried from around the valley either side of the reservoirs – it's still possible to see the scars – and just visible poking through the grass like a line drawing, are the scratchy remains of the old village that once housed the 1,200 workers and their families while they built Scar House Reservoir.

Owned by Yorkshire Water, the two enormous lakes (Scar House is the larger of the two) supply Bradford via the Nidd Aqueduct. This is one of the most beautiful parts of Nidderdale to spend some time in; I love the circular walk around the reservoirs (see box, pages 142–43), where the view is constantly changing, as well as the light. Sheep hug the hillsides and stone walls criss-cross the landscape, the rough grasses and heathers providing a shelter for wildlife. Angram tends to be the livelier of the two, the wind whipping across the water that lashes at the dam wall. On the other side, with the river still only a trickle, Scar House is calmer. Its banks are shallower and have beach-like edges. From the top of the dam, you can look out over the wall to see just how high up you are (216 feet)

"I love the circular walk around the reservoirs, where the view is constantly changing, as well as the light."

Scar House & Angram reservoirs circular walk

❄ OS Explorer map OL20; start: Scar House Reservoir car park, grid reference SE066767.

Beginning at the car park and toilets on the southeastern point of **Scar House Reservoir**, follow the tarmac track (owned by Yorkshire Water) that runs along the southern side. This section is popular with families as the walking is flat and easy, and children can zoom up and down on their bikes; it's also accessible for wheelchairs.

Continue past the end of Scar House Reservoir until you come to the Angram Dam where there's a small hut for shelter – watch out for sheep dung on the seats, woolly beasts shelter in it too!

from the valley floor; it does look a long way down especially when you realise that you are looking into the top branches of the deep green pine trees of Scar Plantation below, which hides some of the drowned village.

1 MIDDLESMOOR, HOW STEAN GORGE & LOFTHOUSE

Middlesmoor is the most far-reaching village along the Nidderdale Valley; there is no other habitation beyond except the odd lonely farmstead. To reach it by road, you need to climb the one-in-four gradient, for the village is perched on top of a hummock, the 15th-century church of St Chad with its castellated square tower acting as a guiding beacon to onlookers.

For a longer walk (an additional 2¼ miles) carry on along the shore of **Angram Reservoir** and keep following the route around its edge until you arrive on the other side of Angram Dam. This additional section has some rough and boggy ground and crosses two bridges over rivers.

Sticking to the Scar House circular walk, cross over the Angram Dam walkway, admiring the views across Angram Reservoir to both Great and Little Whernside. At the northern end of the dam, turn right and follow the path, now with grass under your feet rather than tarmac, along the upper reaches of Scar House Reservoir. It's from here that I think you get some of the best views of the reservoir and the valley running downstream, gaining a real impression of the remoteness of the area.

Cross over a stream and continue along the well-trodden path until you come to a ladder stile and a gate. You can either turn right downhill and then left to wander along the shore of the reservoir or you can climb over the stile on your left and turn almost immediately right to follow the bumpy stone track that runs parallel with the reservoir below you. I prefer this route because you get better views along the valley both in front and behind when you turn around for a passing glance from whence you came.

Arriving at the northern tip of the Scar House Dam, cross over the top of the dam to return to the start, not forgetting to look over the top of the dam wall for a glimpse of the valley floor below. The walk is four miles in total (just over six including a trek around Angram) and is a good family walk – my three children, all under ten, managed it convincingly.

The alternative route to Middlesmoor is via the **Nidderdale Way**. Coming from the north you can pick up the walk at the southeast corner of Scar House Reservoir (close to the car park) and follow the path over In Moor. There's a punishing climb up the very rocky crag to begin but once on top of the moor, the scenery is amply rewarding. As the reservoir disappears from view behind, the moor pans out, the purple heather in late summer an electrifying colour against a shiny blue sky. From here, the path cuts straight across the moor above the village giving views along the progressively greener Nidderdale Valley towards Gouthwaite Reservoir.

"There's a punishing climb to begin but once on top of the moor, the scenery is amply rewarding."

There are some wonderfully poetic names in this area. Look on a large-scale Ordnance Survey map and you come across places like Foggyshaw Barn, Limley Pastures, Beggar Moat Scar and Goyden Pot. Next on the list of fanciful names is Hard Gap Lane, close to the village of Stean. Actually Stean is no more than a few houses but what makes it famous is **How Stean Gorge**. This vast ravine with umpteen geological features is indeed impressive as a natural attraction, the waters of the How Stean Beck tumbling over giant boulders and smoothing the limestone into bizarre creations as it flows through the towering gap before wending its way to join the River Nidd. It's impressive enough to warrant SSSI status, but frankly I found the entrance fee less than impressive – or rather impressively high. I'd prefer to avoid the fee and instead glimpse the gorge from the various footpaths, including the Nidderdale Way, that run alongside – and across – the beck.

"The views towards the green pastures dotted with trees and the higher fells behind will leave a lasting impression on the mind."

The first village to actually straddle the Nidd is **Lofthouse**, a good starting point for a number of walks, including a footpath that runs right alongside the Nidd. A short cut narrow road across Masham Moor to the village of Masham also begins at Lofthouse. Even if you have no plans to go right across the moor (a nicely rugged and bleak stamping ground) take a moment to climb the steep **Trapping Hill** out of Lofthouse and look back along the valley towards Gouthwaite in the southeast and further round towards the hummock of Middlesmoor in the northwest. The views towards the green pastures dotted with trees and the higher fells behind will leave a lasting impression on the mind.

¶¶ FOOD & DRINK

Useful for walkers is the **Crown Hotel** in the tiny village square in Middlesmoor (✆ 01423 755204), welcoming with autumnal log fires on a frosty day. Lofthouse has its own pub, also confusingly called the **Crown Hotel** (✆ 01423 755206). Both pubs serve ales brewed by the Black Sheep Brewery at Masham.

2 RAMSGILL, GOUTHWAITE RESERVOIR & WATH

Of all the villages in Upper Nidderdale, **Ramsgill** is the jewel. It sits at the northern head of Gouthwaite Reservoir, a grouping of comfortably proportioned stone cottages. The houses are centred around a large, immaculately kept green and a harmonious church. At its head is the striking old shooting lodge that is now the Yorke Arms, iced with ivy. Also in the village is the Ramsgill Studio (✆ 01423 755098 ⌖ www. ramsgillstudio.co.uk), a small art and craft gallery exhibiting and selling work from various artists including the owner Sarah Garforth, who specialises in painting scenes of Nidderdale. Sarah also runs small and intimate workshops in her studio for painters of all abilities (or none!). It's hard to say whether such beautiful surroundings will prove inspirational or distracting.

"The houses are centred around a large, immaculately kept green and a harmonious church. At its head is the striking old shooting lodge that is now the Yorke Arms, iced with ivy."

This village too, makes a good base for a walk, the Ramsgill Beck playfully splitting the village in two, the halves joined by a tiny bridge. Wander over a second bridge that crosses the Nidd a little north of Ramsgill and follow the road to the hamlet of **Bouthwaite**. From there, on slightly higher ground, you get wonderful views towards Ramsgill with the River Nidd and Gouthwaite Reservoir in the foreground. You'll also cross the ghostly tracks of the old railway that once plied the workers building Angram and Scar House reservoirs with materials.

Gouthwaite Reservoir, also supplying Bradford with water, is not a bit like its more northerly cousins. This one is long, sleek and dark, where the movement of the water is minimal except on the stormiest of days. At its head, close to Ramsgill, the reedy banks provide housing for nesting waterfowl while, two-thirds along the western side, a platform has been set up for birdwatchers to sit and view the mannerisms of the native and migrating wildlife that call the reservoir home, if only for a season.

The Nidderdale Way follows right along both sides of the reservoir while the Dales Explorer Bus (see page 17) stops opposite the viewing platform at weekends. There's also a pleasant picnic spot across the road, next to a small and unobtrusive car park.

At the southern end of Gouthwaite Reservoir lies the tiny hamlet of **Wath**, again just a few houses, this time spread out like beads along a ribbon above the river. The Nidd flows past, the Nidderdale Way following it.

🍴 FOOD & DRINK

Sportsman's Arms Hotel Wath HG3 5PP 📞 01423 711306 📠 www.sportsmans-arms.
co.uk. Fantastic location and a beautiful building both inside and out; the gardens, adjacent
to the river, make the most of the surrounding scenery. Reservations recommended for the
restaurant. Accommodation too.

Yorke Arms Ramsgill HG3 5RL 📞 01423 755243 📠 www.yorke-arms.co.uk. Winner of
several foodie awards, including a Michelin star. Accommodation too.

3 PATELEY BRIDGE

🏠 **Bewerley Hall Cottage**, Bewerley (see page 177)

For many visitors to the area, Nidderdale begins and ends at Pateley
Bridge. It's as if they arrive in the town, and leave without going any
further up the valley. Oh, what they miss, but Pateley Bridge is a very
good start.

The small town is flanked on both sides by the sharply rising,
beautifully green, fells on either side, the Nidd adding a very pretty
decoration to the town's beauty. It is Nidderdale's gateway – there is no
other route to Upper Nidderdale other than through the town – so it
remains an important 'capital' to both visitors and local communities
alike. Pateley Bridge is home to the annual **Nidderdale Show** (📠 www.
nidderdaleshow.co.uk), a major rural event in the area's calendar, held
every autumn in Bewerley Park. It is a fantastic day that, perhaps more
than anything else, epitomises the beating heart of Nidderdale and what
it means to live and work in the area.

Much of Pateley's interest lines the High Street which rises steeply
from the bridge over the River Nidd that gives the town its name – a
quaint assemblage of little shops and eateries leaning on each other's
shoulders as they climb the hill. Among these is **The Oldest Sweet Shop
in England** (📠 www.oldestsweetshop.co.uk), on the corner of Church
Street, with one of the largest selections of old-fashioned teeth-rotters
and filling-pullers you're likely to find anywhere. Personally I can never
resist the sherbert lemons.

The Old Workhouse

King Street, HG3 5LE 📠 www.theoldworkhouse.org.

Up the hill from the town centre, this austere Victorian building is now
home to a range of enterprises. The **Nidderdale Museum** (📞 01423
711225 📠 www.nidderdalemuseum.com) catalogues the grim goings-on

in the building's past among other things. It is an absolute gem, run by volunteers and a bargain for families – children accompanied by parents enter free of charge, hence our two-hour family visit cost a couple of quid. At first, the museum appears ever so slightly stuffy with a few items from the olden days pinned up on a wall with others displayed in a glass cabinet – but from here, it simply gets better, as visitors become drawn into the fascinating world of Nidderdale life. Each exhibition is split into themed rooms exactly as you would anticipate finding them – the cobbler's shop, the joiner's shop, agriculture room, Victorian parlour, workhouse and general store all bring the area to life, with implements and exhibits donated by local people. Set aside at least an hour, but don't be surprised if you find yourself there for considerably longer.

The **Nidderdale Area of Outstanding Natural Beauty office** has lots of information on the walls about the AONB, its geology and environment, and also posted are details of countryside events throughout the year, from pond dipping to dragonfly walks, volunteer fence building to acorn collecting, and guided walks.

The **King Street Workshops** and **Number 6 Studio Gallery** form the building's creative hub, giving space to six craftsmen and women plus an exhibition area where art courses take place.

Coldstones Cut

Coldstones Quarry, Greenhow Hills HG3 5JQ   0845 600 6616   http://thecoldstonescut.org. This is a staggering place in more ways than one, as you have to walk nearly half a mile and climb 150 feet, from Toft House car park, to even see it. When you get there though, what you see will take what's left of your breath away. It is the biggest sculpture in Yorkshire – a monumental piece of public art that allows you to scale a series of platforms and view the huge working quarry below, and Nidderdale in the distance. From an original idea in 2006 by the quarry's owners, Hanson Aggregates, it took the designer Andrew Sabin three years to complete before its opening in 2010.

FOOD & DRINK

The Crown High St   01423 712455   www.thecrowninn-pateleybridge.co.uk. A classic High Street pub – the only one remaining in fact, but good for all that.

Elliot's 31 High St   01423 711851   www.elliotsdeli.co.uk. Splendid deli serving all kinds of typically deli things including many local products. Perfect for putting a picnic together.

The Willow Restaurant Park Rd ✆ 01423 711689 🖰 www.thewillowpateley.co.uk. Just off the High Street, down a tiny alley. I've been going to this restaurant for years and have never been disappointed.

EASTERN NIDDERDALE

East of Pateley Bridge, the land doesn't exactly flatten out but it's not quite so harsh and inhospitable. The hills and valleys begin to look vividly green, the stone walls that turn the hills into pastures, creating geometric patterns, all the more noticeable. Due east of Pateley Bridge is the extraordinary geological spectacle of **Brimham Rocks**. North and south of these mammoth natural sculptures are two clusters of villages. Some of these villages, in the southern cluster, lie in the Nidd's valley

NIDDERDALE LLAMAS

Kiln Farm, Wilsill, Pateley Bridge HG3 5EF ✆ 01423 711052 🖰 www.nidderdalellamas.org.

I first met Jack and Ike when they were three years old, Ike likened to a stroppy teenager despite his age. Louis was a little younger, just two years old, while Ted was the baby at 15 months, desperately trying to be more grown up like his friends. This is not the result of something in the Nidderdale water, creating a male baby boom at the hands of Suzanne Benson, though these are her babies of a sort. These are her llamas, reared and trained for pack trekking through some of the most inspirational countryside you're ever likely to see in England while with a llama. And if there is ever a perfect way to take things slowly, this has to be it.

Nidderdale Llamas is based at Kiln Farm in Wilsill, a tiny hillside village between Pateley Bridge and Summerbridge. It's run by Suzanne Benson who fell head-over-hooves in love with llamas when she discovered their

intelligent and loving character. I discovered this character too when I took Jack and Ike out for a walk on one of Suzanne's llama treks through Nidderdale.

You don't ride llamas, but you walk with them and they carry your stuff while they amble along at the pace set by you – and sometimes by them should they find an irresistible blade or two of grass to eat on the way. I found it to be one of the most gentle and sociable ways to explore the countryside, strolling at a pace far slower than I would go during a normal hike across the hills. Having first met the llamas in their own environment and been given the opportunity to handle them before setting out on our walk, I felt confident that I knew their personalities a little bit. That tiny speck of knowledge grew into a real bond with Jack and Ike, my llamas for the day, tucked up against the sides of the river; others cling like limpets to the sides of the hills. The northern cluster, centred around **Galphay** and **Kirkby Malzeard**, lie in the Nidderdale AONB but the streams and rivulets that drift through them link up with the River Ure, after its journey through Wensleydale.

4 BRIMHAM ROCKS

If there is ever a place to take children for some good old-fashioned life-building skills, **Brimham Rocks** is it. Sure, it may well frighten parents, anxiously watching as their children hurtle from one giant stack of boulders to the next oblivious to the potential pitfalls – literally – but it is a breath of fresh air to find a place where nature prevails and children can pretty much do as they please. They can stand and climb without

something that is quite common as Suzanne explained during our trek.

'Llamas are very intelligent creatures. They will look you up and down (indeed they did), weigh you up as to whether they can be mischievous while in your care and will work with you as you walk. They are very easy to handle. We have had a very elderly woman who came to trek with the llamas and likewise, a wheelchair-bound visitor who was blind. There was something about the llamas' instinct, they could sense that they needed to be even more gentle and considerate than they usually are and the visitors, despite their immobility, found a true bond with their llamas.'

Kiln Farm is high on a hill and looks straight across the dale. Other than short walks around the farm, the llamas are trekked along footpaths and bridleways in the area. It's great to be able to learn about the animals as you trek and, because of the slow pace, Suzanne can point out all the beauty of the Dales as you go. Part way through the trek, the llamas are given their break and you get the refreshments that they have been so considerately carrying. One of the longer trekking options is to Brimham Rocks.

Suzanne tailors each trek according to the people that are booked. Therefore, it is not possible to simply turn up to the farm unannounced either to look at the llamas (the chances are, they won't be there) or to expect a trek immediately. It's not advisable for children under ten years to trek with a llama because of the pace ('young children tend to get bored with the slow speed,' says Suzanne) but children from the age of 12 will easily be able to lead a llama, so long as they have an accompanying adult with them. Don't be surprised if you find yourself talking to the animals!

red tape and risk assessments, and appreciate the magnificence, and significance, of the landscape without 'Don't' signs littering the place; the only warning is that things might be a bit slippery and you need to be aware of sudden drops.

With my children we've had magical times there jumping, climbing, respecting and appreciating. These giant stacks of millstone grit, carved by glaciation, erosion and any amount of geological disturbances over more years than one can contemplate, certainly

"With my children we've had magical times there jumping, climbing, respecting and appreciating."

focus the imagination and they make fantastic climbing frames. Perched nearly 1,000 feet above sea level on the heather-cloaked Brimham Moor, they also provide primeval-feeling views across Nidderdale. The area around the rocks is designated an SSSI for its surrounding plant life. Secret paths dart this way and that, the bracken and the rowan trees fighting for space, their late summer show of red berries exploding with colour against the lichen-covered darkness of the rocky giants.

The National Trust owns the site and entrance is free, with just a small charge for parking (free for NT members); there's a small refreshment kiosk on site. You can access the rocks at weekends by using the Dales Explorer Bus (see page 17) from Pateley Bridge; the Nidderdale Way passes over Brimham Moor too.

5 RIPLEY

As the Nidd runs its course towards Knaresborough, the dale broadens, turning from bleak moorland to shallow hills dotted with farmsteads and small villages. This is perhaps the kind of landscape that most would associate with the Dales – a gentle river of no great size and a rolling countryside of emerald green that's broken up by stone walls built to a Dales spec.

Ripley, three miles north of Harrogate, is one village that surpasses all others in this area as a magnet for visitors. The signs at its edge announce Ripley lays claim to a famous ice cream. Actually it's **Ripley Castle** (01423 770152 www.ripleycastle.co.uk) for which the place is famous, the rather beautiful home of the Ingilby family, taking centre place within the small, estate-owned village. While the interior is attractive and the associations with British history are impressive, it's the exterior that appeals to me: the walled gardens with their huge herbaceous borders, the kitchen garden full of rare varieties of fruit trees and the pleasure grounds, with two shapely lakes, silted up from a beck that runs into the nearby Nidd.

The grounds have that archetypal estate feel, planted with specimen trees that defy age. Giant wellingtonia reach for the sky alongside oaks and sweet chestnut trees vying for the biggest and knobbliest girth competition, their trunks showing more warts and pimples than the foulest of imaginary characters.

On your way out, take a peek inside **All Saints' Church**. It has the most beautiful ceiling decorated like a piece of fabric with a repeat pattern in simple reds and greens, embossed with gold. It couldn't be simpler but is all the better for it.

¶¶ FOOD & DRINK

The Boar's Head Hotel HG3 3AY ✆ 01423 771888 ⌂ www.boarsheadripley.co.uk. Housed in a fine building (note the arched windows) in the centre of the village. Refined dining in either the restaurant or the bistro. Sir Thomas Ingilby, owner of Ripley Castle, personally selects the wines for the wine list.

KNARESBOROUGH & HARROGATE

6 KNARESBOROUGH

It's hard to tell what is the dominant feature of Knaresborough, a town that perches on a steep bank above the River Nidd. Is it the river itself, the huge viaduct (potentially the best-known feature as its vista is regularly used to promote the town), the ruined castle that just about stands above the river, or is it actually the town's most famous and oldest tourist attraction, Mother Shipton's Cave, tucked away out of sight?

Most of the town sits to one side of the Nidd. On the other are the remains of the Ancient Forest of Knaresborough. The woods, which include hornbeams, oak, ash and beech trees that smell like peaches when you wander through them, screen **Mother Shipton's Cave** and the bizarre well that turns everything to stone – including numerous hanging teddy bears, and has been drawing visitors since the early 17th century. The beech trees are considered to be such fine specimens that every one has a preservation order placed upon it and the Forestry Commission has filed a seed bank for future plantings. You do have to pay to wander through the woods (accessed at the entrance to Mother Shipton's Cave) but, running alongside the river, there's an arresting view of the town and a nice picnic spot too.

On entering Knaresborough, either by train over the **viaduct** high above the river – what an eye-opening introduction to the town – or other means, I think the most prominent feature is actually the number of **black-and-white chequered buildings**. It's a significant trademark of the town and the mysterious reason behind them all makes it all the more intriguing. I've received all kinds of answers when enquiring around the town, including some kind of relationship with the chequered flag used to signal the end of a grand prix! But the most plausible answer is likely to be that the checks used to denote licensed premises (hence pub names like 'The Chequers Inn'); consequently in Knaresborough, it then became fashionable to paint your house black and white, explaining why there are so many. Oddly, these mono houses look right, yet could you imagine if anyone tried to paint their house similarly elsewhere? There could be uproar among neighbours.

"It's a significant trademark of the town and the mysterious reason behind them all makes it all the more intriguing. I've received all kinds of answers when enquiring around the town, including some kind of relationship with the chequered flag used to signal the end of a grand prix!"

Close to the river, and the viaduct, is one of these chequered houses, the **Old Manor House**. Built in the 12th century, it is where King Charles I and Oliver Cromwell signed the treaty that ended the English Civil War. The ancient **Knaresborough Castle**, positioned high above a bend in the river, played its part in the war too, with a parliamentary siege on the Royalist camp. It is now officially owned by the Queen, although an overnight stay by Her Majesty in this tumbledown residence might not have quite the same appeal that it once had for many of her forbears. It is, however, the best place to snap a photo of the most traditional of Knaresborough scenes, overlooking the river and the viaduct.

Wandering along **Waterside**, naturally by the river, you begin to get a real feel for the town, a tiered system of beautiful terraced houses each with a miniature garden. You can hire a rowing boat here too, to appreciate the river from another perspective. There are several options to reach the main town area from Waterside but they all involve a good

KNARESBOROUGH BED RACE

Knaresborough is famed for its annual Bed Race (⌂ www.knaresborough.co.uk/bedrace), a real community-spirited athletic event with the subtle difference of pushing a decorated bed through the streets! It might not make it as an Olympic sport, but at least there is somewhere to snooze after all the strenuous activity. It's usually held every June, and most competitors take a dip in the Nidd during the closing stages of the race.

climb, including the steep steps up to the castle, from where you can see the old mill on the opposite side of the river. The fields around Knaresborough used to be filled with the daily flourish of hazy blue flax and the mill was appointed by Queen Victoria to supply linen for all the royal palaces.

The old town is centred around the **marketplace**, still in weekly use for the Wednesday sales, and the **High Street**. I love the centre. It has higgledy-piggledy house roofs and narrow streets that radiate from the centre like spokes on a wheel. Look out for some unusual windows around the town; the 'Town Windows' project is a recent collection of public art that uses the *trompe l'œil* effect – at first glance you'll believe that someone really is hanging out of a window. That someone is actually one of 12 characters from the town's past and they're used to brighten up some of the blank windows in the town's Georgian buildings.

One of these historical figures is Blind Jack. Born in 1717, Jack Metcalf lost his sight as a child through smallpox yet went on to become a reputed fiddle player and a pioneer in civil engineering, constructing 180 miles of roads throughout Yorkshire. He can be seen playing his fiddle from an upstairs window in the pub that bears his name, in the market square. But you can also sit next to him, again in the marketplace, where the bronze figure of Blind Jack rests on a bench, his measuring wheel propped up by his side.

One of Knaresborough's more contemporary places to visit is **Henshaws Arts and Crafts Centre** (⌂ www.henshaws.org.uk) on Bond End (the A59 towards Harrogate). This complex has a circular brick turret-like entrance sandwiched between high stone walls, which makes it feel as if you're entering through a castle keep. Inside there are shops selling crafts made by visually impaired residents of Yorkshire, a wonderful sensory garden that can be appreciated and enjoyed by all, and a gallery café. The centre also runs a whole range of arts workshops that anyone can join.

A wander down to the River Nidd and along Abbey Road follows the river for a mile (actually coming to a dead end) past private riverside gardens; the peace is sublime while the town continues daily life on a clifftop above. This is actually the ancient Pilgrim's Way and tucked back into the rock is one of the sweetest, tiniest chapels that you will come across, the 600-year-old **Chapel of Our Lady of the Crag**. Look for too long at the river and you'll miss it, the powder-blue door is its only clue of existence. Beside it is a beautiful rock garden and it is, I believe, the most restful place to sit in the town.

￼ FOOD & DRINK

For its size, Knaresborough is blessed with more than its fair share of good pubs, at least ten of which serve locally brewed cask beer. A short stroll from the railway station along the High Street, down Cheapside and Briggate and back along the riverside, passes pretty much all of them so you can take your pick. Three that stand out are **Blind Jack's** on the marketplace for its cosy ambience, **The Cross Keys** on Cheapside (especially on Monday pie night) and **The Dropping Well Inn** by Low Bridge for its historic Mother Shipton and Guy Fawkes connections. Other notable places to eat and drink include:

Becket's Restaurant and Grill Castlegate ￼ 01423 869918 ￼ www.becketsrestaurant. co.uk. Not cheap but the food is very good and almost entirely locally sourced.

Riverside Café Waterside ￼ 01423 546759. No-nonsense dog-friendly café in a great location.

7 HARROGATE

Where York has history and Knaresborough has small-world charm, Harrogate has elegance. My father used to say that it was easy to imagine Miss Marple-like elderly spinster ladies daintily sipping tea out of bone china cups and nibbling on cucumber sandwiches while discussing society life. Even today the centre of Harrogate is about refinement.

Harrogate's appearance owes much to the kind of visitors it has been able to attract over the centuries – wealthy and noble society from across Europe in search of cures for ailments from the town's spa water. They brought money into the area and with it an air of decadence. Today the town regularly features on top ten lists of the best places to live.

The vast open expanse right in the centre of town is **The Stray**, an important part of Harrogate community life where joggers breathe a cleaner air, and any number of weekend football matches for all ages take place. An act of parliament created the park in the late 18th century, fixing its size at 200 acres, which must be maintained today.

HARROGATE FLOWER SHOWS

With such a floral tradition, Harrogate is renowned too for hosting one of the most important events in the gardening calendar, particularly in the north. The spring (in April) and autumn (in September) Flower shows (www.flowershow.org.uk), held at the Great Yorkshire Showground, attract thousands of gardeners who return home from the shows laden with plants and having filled their heads with advice from specialist plant societies and gardening experts.

Unless you're planning on purchasing a lorry-load of plants, you can travel to the showground by shuttle bus directly from the town centre, running from Station Parade.

There's no doubt that it enhances the look of Harrogate and in winter, when the trees that line its perimeter twinkle with fairy lights, it takes on a magical quality.

Floral Harrogate

Harrogate is renowned for its gardens. The town regularly wins national and regional awards for its floral displays and the volunteer organisation behind it, **Harrogate in Bloom** (www.harrogateinbloom.org.uk), has a wealth of community projects to ensure that everyone, of all ages, can take part and be proud of their success. The team has created **Harrogate's Floral Trail** (www.moguide.com), a marked route with a sound guide that you can download on to your mobile, iPod or MP3 player. The route takes in 11 public gardens, including the most famous promenading spot of them all, the **Valley Gardens**. The year-round colour here is more than vibrant, a classic spa-town garden with giant specimen trees, lawns and flower borders that show true dedication from their gardeners. Seasonal displays of autumn crocus and dahlias are replaced with bird-enticing (their presence ever-heard through their birdsong) deep red holly berries, jungle plants hover above streamlets and alpine rockeries make way for formal rose beds, while a giant and ancient wisteria slithers its gnarled trunk

"The year-round colour here is more than vibrant, a classic spa-town garden with giant specimen trees, lawns and flower borders that show true dedication from their gardeners."

up the pillars of a walkway like a serpent. One footpath through the gardens is named the **Elgar Route**. It commemorates Sir Edward Elgar's love of Harrogate; he visited many times from 1912 to 1927 and would walk regularly in the Valley Gardens. The first provincial performance of the composer's Second Symphony was held in the town in 1911.

There's another garden of significance in Harrogate, the Royal Horticultural Society's northern home at **Harlow Carr**. It's huge and shows all the professionalism that you would expect from the nation's largest gardening organisation. However it is also a trial site, where plants and gardening techniques are assessed for their suitability in a northern climate. It's in danger of becoming an all-singing-all-dancing theme park rather than concentrating on gardening but the stunning contemporary acclimatised alpine greenhouse and a Learning Centre (built from sustainable materials and with a zero carbon footprint) should keep Harlow Carr special. Bus 106 goes to Harlow Carr from Station Parade; visitors arriving at the gardens by bus receive half-price entry. Alternatively you can take the very pleasant 1½-mile marked walk through the Valley Gardens and Harrogate's **Pinewoods**, a woodland that's filled with sycamore, birch and rowan as well as pine trees.

A spa town

Tewitt Well, the original iron and sulphur-rich spring that began Harrogate's fortunes as a spa town, is found within The Stray but other locations around the town also have waters bubbling up from the deep.

"The sulphurous spa water tastes absolutely disgusting (by which token we can assume it's good for you)."

One such place is the **Royal Pump Room**, the refined-looking black and gold building close to the Valley Gardens. It houses a museum exhibiting the history of the town as a spa and you can drink a glass of what is allegedly Europe's most sulphurous spa water if you feel you must. It tastes absolutely disgusting (by which token we can assume it's good for you) and a sulphurous smell pervades the air outside.

Close by, the **Turkish Baths and Health Spa**, (☎ 01423 556746 ⌂ www.turkishbathsharrogate.co.uk) is the place to unwind in the same way that society did in the 19th century, though with a few modern alterations and luxuries. Restored in 2004, the baths are one of the most historically complete of their kind remaining in Britain. With a Moorish design, the Islamic arches, decorated pillars, glazed brickwork walls, painted ceilings and terrazzo floors are a work of art and that's before you've dipped a toe into the plunge pool or laid your head on a soft pillow in the rest room.

You can simply turn up on to use the Turkish baths but it's worth booking one of the many spa treatments for a truly rejuvenating experience.

Bettys & Taylors of Harrogate

The very first thing that comes into my head when I think of Yorkshire is **Bettys**, a Yorkshire institution. It is a world-renowned family empire of elegant tea rooms and a few other things beside. Although now very much a 'Yorkshire thing', the story actually began in Switzerland. Orphaned under tragic circumstances, a young Fritz Bützer, the son of a Swiss miller and master-baker, came to England in 1907 to find work. Getting on to the wrong train in London, he found himself in Bradford without the means to return. After many years of hard work and dedication to learn the art of chocolate making, and a certain amount of moving around Yorkshire, he anglicised his name to Frederick Belmont, moved to Harrogate and opened a café with only the finest-quality furnishings and serving the finest-quality food and drink, with the finest service. All this finery encouraged high-society visitors.

"Bettys is owned and run by Frederick Belmont's nephew Jonathan Wild, together with his wife Lesley. There are now six tea rooms in Harrogate, York, Ilkley and Northallerton, each with a very special, individual character and ambience."

Ninety years on, Bettys is owned and run by Frederick Belmont's nephew Jonathan Wild, together with his wife Lesley. There are now six tea rooms in Harrogate, York, Ilkley and Northallerton, each with a very special, individual character and ambience. Having bought out the long-time tea and coffee merchants, **Taylors of Harrogate** (world-famous for 'Yorkshire Tea'), in the 1960s, every aspect of the Bettys business today is maintained with the highest standards. For example, in the craft bakery where all the Bettys products are made, housed in a beautiful 'Swiss chalet' in Harrogate, every process is done by hand, whether it's making speciality breads ready for baking in the traditional brick oven, creating the most divine cakes, tarts and biscuits or making the very finest chocolates.

I paid a visit to **Bettys Cookery School**, (Hookstone Park ✆ 01423 814016 🖰 www.bettyscookeryschool.co.uk) based opposite Bettys craft bakery in Harrogate. It was set up by Lesley Wild in 2001 and has the enviable resource of being able to draw on the talents of the craftsmen, bakers, confectioners and cooks who work for Bettys. They still look to their Swiss–Yorkshire heritage for inspiration and it's this that really makes the courses unique and inspiring.

I joined in with the school's pinnacle course, the ten-day 'Bettys Certificate Course', which covers just about everything you need to know for a really firm grounding in cooking, from knife skills and pastry techniques to chocolate making, taught by one of the master chocolatiers from Bettys bakery.

"Friendliness abounds but they are helpful and non-judgemental too, turning the most nervous, or newest, of cooks into confident cooks."

The school kitchen is incredible, a room that is inspiring to cook in before the lovely staff have even said a word. However, it is the warmth of the tutors that make the school and the teaching so special. Friendliness abounds but they are helpful and non-judgemental too, turning the most nervous, or newest, of cooks into confident cooks. The most experienced of chefs will gain something from one of their cookery courses too, even if it's simply a fantastic day out and meeting new friends. Of the 'pupils' on the Certificate Course that I attended, some were local to the area while others had made it their holiday in Yorkshire and were full of praise for the school. With breakfast, lunch and dinner thrown in, who could ask for more? The school is also very keen to encourage young cooks. Said Richard Jones, the cookery school manager who pops around to chat while you're cooking. 'Inspiring children to cook is one of the main reasons that Lesley Wild wanted to set up the school. We offer courses that will ensure that children can cook a proper meal, not simply fairy cakes'.

Personally, I can't wait to return for other practical one-day courses – anything from preparing supper parties, and pasta making (I need to hone the skills that I learned on the last course), to cooking with chocolate. But there are two that really grab my eye. One is entitled the 'Flavours of Switzerland', taking students back to Bettys roots. The other is 'Yorkshire Breads', learning to bake traditional loaves and pikelets. I can't think of a better souvenir of Yorkshire.

Harrogate & art

While its sulphurous waters have brought fame to the town, its connections with the arts are lesser known, although one rather famous crime writer did put Harrogate in the headlines. The **Old Swan Hotel**, close to the Valley Gardens, was the bolt-hole for Agatha Christie in 1926. A nationwide search for the author was launched following her disappearance but she was found ten days later having checked into the hotel under a pseudonym. It was a plot to match any of her thrillers, involving secret affairs, revenge and the possibility of murder; the mystery remains as to why she chose to disappear, but it was possibly revenge against her husband who had just announced his secret affair with another woman – her disappearance cast suspicious rumours that he had murdered her.

"It was a plot to match any of her thrillers, involving secret affairs, revenge and the possibility of murder; the mystery remains as to why she chose to disappear, but it was possibly revenge against her husband. "

Between the hotel and the Valley Gardens is the **Mercer Art Gallery** on Swan Road (✆ 01423 556188 ◌ www.harrogate.gov.uk/mercerartgallery). This neoclassical building is home to Harrogate's fine art collection of 2,000 works, although these are not on permanent display. It's only a small gallery, free to enter, and exhibitions change regularly. On display are works by local artists, photography, national touring exhibitions and themed displays of prints, paintings and drawings taken from the permanent collection.

To enjoy art and the company of others, the **Nidd Valley Decorative and Fine Arts Society** (◌ www.niddvalleydfas.org.uk) holds monthly lectures on a wide range of themes and subjects, using experienced and knowledgeable public speakers. Sally Wilks, Chairman of the Society, explained: 'We are always delighted to welcome and involve people who are only staying in the vicinity for a short time and who enjoy art. The talks are always informative and are a wonderful way of meeting like-minded people.' Informal lectures are held every third Monday of the month at Christchurch Centre on The Stray; a small donation is requested per visitor.

¶ FOOD & DRINK

Bettys Café Tearoom 1–3 Parliament St ✆ 01423 502746 ◌ www.bettysandtaylors. co.uk. The ultimate dining experience in Harrogate, even if it's just for a cup of tea while listening to the resident pianist or people-watching through the plate-glass windows. Visit the Montpellier Bar (closest to the entrance) for a quick, continental-style menu of open sandwiches and tortes from the bar, or the main tea rooms for full-blown at-table service and a more traditional tea room menu (that includes some Swiss favourites too of course). For a fantastic cup of tea, you can't beat the Tearoom Blend. It's not the cheapest place in town, but you're paying for the whole ambience as well as top-quality food. Freshly made breads, cakes and biscuits as well as Taylors' teas and coffees can be bought in the shop too.

Deano's Graze and Grill Oxford St ✆ 01423 505300 🖮 www.grazeandgrill.co.uk. One of many very good restaurants in the town. A sort of Yorkshire tapas venue.

Drum and Monkey Montpellier Gardens ✆ 01423 502650 🖮 www.drumandmonkey. co.uk. Atmospheric little restaurant specialising in really good seafood.

Farrah's Food Hall 31 Montpellier Parade ✆ 01423 525266 🖮 www.farrahs.com. Farrah's are the makers of Harrogate Toffee, a delicious slightly lemony-flavoured toffee that was originally created to take the rather yucky taste of the sulphurous spa water away. Their food hall sells all their toffees, fudges and a whole host of other sweets.

The Fat Badger White Hart Hotel, Coldbath Rd ✆ 01423 505681 🖮 www.thefatbadger. co.uk. Harrogate is not renowned for its pubs but this one within the White Hart Hotel deserves a mention for the range and quality of both food and beers.

Fodder Great Yorkshire Showground, HG2 8NZ ✆ 01423 546111 🖮 www.fodderweb.co.uk. This fantastic farm shop is owned by the Yorkshire Agricultural Society; 85% of the products on sale are made, baked or grown in Yorkshire. There's an environmental and sustainable ethos behind the whole business from the new building to educating children on where food comes from. There's a great café on-site too.

Hales Bar Crescent Rd ✆ 01423 725570 🖮 www.halesbar.co.uk. The oldest pub in Harrogate and it looks it (in the best possible sense). Edwardian décor and original gas lighting, and great food and drink.

Weetons 23/24 West Park ✆ 01423 507100 🖮 www.weetons.com. Weetons describe themselves as 'the farm shop in the town', opposite The Stray. Owned by local farmers, it's a fantastic deli, butchers and bakery selling lots of Yorkshire produce including Ampleforth cider and a Triple Curd Cheese, made from their own dairy herd. There's also a good, bustling café on-site.

NORTH FROM HARROGATE TO MASHAM

While the A1 carves up North Yorkshire, slicing between the Yorkshire Dales and the North York Moors, the Ure Valley to the west is far from dull with a string of attractive properties, market towns and satellite villages making the most of their rural location.

HOLY PLACES

From pagan holy wells and Buddhist meditation centres to medieval abbeys and Friends meeting houses, the Yorkshire Dales are rich in sacred places for many religious persuasions.

1 The serene ruins of Fountains Abbey. (ss) 2 Bolton Abbey, Wharfedale, one of Britain's most intact priories. (s/J) 3 St Michael's Church in Linton dates from the 12th century. (JF)

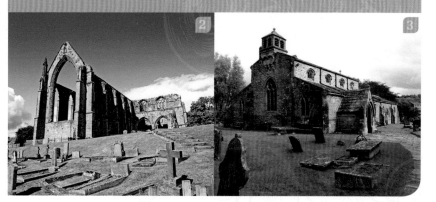

RURAL COMMUNITY

The village is the beating heart of Dales life. It's where you will find the shop, the pub and sometimes even the railway station. They may be under threat elsewhere, but villages are holding their own here.

1 Settle train station at one end of that famous line. (ss) 2 One of the Dales's many sheep fairs and shows – a chance to catch up with old friends. (PH/AWL) 3 Grassington's brass band in full swing. (C/A) 4 A nice 'Slow' way to get around in Wensleydale. (TS/FL) 5 Muker village shop, which also doubles as a tea room and tourist information centre. (ss) 6 Askrigg, a typical Dales village. (ss) 7 The oldest sweet shop in England, Pateley Bridge. (OSS)

A YORKSHIREMAN'S HOME IS HIS CASTLE

It's testament to less peaceful times that all of the Dales possess at least one castle. Some are mere humps and lumps on the ground, many are stately ruins and one or two still host the occasional battle.

1 Bolton Castle ... or is it Castle Bolton? (BC) 2 Watch out, the Lancastrians are coming! A medieval re-enactment at Skipton Castle. (SC)

8 MARKENFIELD HALL

☎ 01765 692303 ⌂ www.markenfield.com; see website for opening days. Just over a mile off the main A61 and three miles south of Ripon.

One of the best-preserved – and most beautiful – medieval houses in Britain today, Markenfield Hall is most definitely someone's house, and that is why it works its spell on me. With the exception of a spot of tinkering over the centuries, it has remained largely unaltered since it was built in the early 14th century for the de Markenfield family. Completely surrounded by a fashionable moat (it wouldn't keep out many marauding armies!) and walled courtyard, this wonderful crenellated house has seen a remarkable and tragic history, its walls, rooms and tiny chapel playing a major part in the 1569 Rising of the North, a battle in direct rebellion to Henry VIII's dissolution of the monasteries. This caused the house – and the family's – downfall.

> "Completely surrounded by a fashionable moat (it wouldn't keep out many marauding armies!) and walled courtyard, this wonderful crenellated house has seen a remarkable and tragic history."

Today Markenfield Hall is once again owned by descendants of the Markenfield family. They have restored the magnificent Great Hall, winning the Historic Houses Association Restoration Project of the Year in 2008 (beating Harewood House, arguably one of Yorkshire's grandest attractions, in the process). Standing in the courtyard, listening to the history that befell the property while glancing at the giant petals bursting opening on the magnolia that climbs the wall by the entrance way, you can almost hear the whispers and the chatter of disgruntled Catholics plotting against the forwarding armies.

Markenfield Hall's tiny chapel, restored alongside the Great Hall, is unique too, especially given its past history; it is licensed to hold both Catholic and Protestant services, even if there is only room to fit a dozen or so people in the congregation.

The hall is only open to the public on certain afternoons throughout the year, when you can tour the courtyard and four rooms (including the Great Hall and chapel). I really urge you to visit but it's advisable to check the website for opening times. Guided group visits can be booked all year round. The Ripon Rowel Walk runs past the moat and gatehouse. Note there are no refreshments at the hall.

9 FOUNTAINS ABBEY & STUDLEY ROYAL

HD4 3DY ✆ 01765 608888 ◌ www.nationaltrust.org.uk; National Trust.

The remains of the Cistercian foundation of **Fountains Abbey**, four miles southwest of Ripon and just a few fields away from Markenfield Hall, constitute the ultimate romantic ruin. Yes, it would be wonderful to see it as it once stood, but there's a certain charm in willowy grasses and ivy growing out of the roof, wild figs sunning themselves in the abbey courtyard and every crevice and archway stuffed with wild scabious waving in the wind that blows along the valley of the River Skell, and the soothing sound of its waters rushing past the ruins to the adjacent Fountains Mill. The Cistercian monks certainly knew how to pick a good location. We have Henry VIII and his iron will to crush Catholicism to thank (if you can really use the word) for the flora and being able to watch the birds flutter in and out under the vaulted arches of the old refectory. There's a steep climb beyond the river valley but take a wander up to the secret lookout named Anne Boleyn's Seat (is that title given in jest with a hint of irony?) and you'll appreciate all the more how magnificent the abbey would once have been.

"It would be wonderful to see it as it once stood, but there's a certain charm in willowy grasses, ivy growing out of the roof, and wild figs sunning themselves in the abbey courtyard."

From Anne Boleyn's Seat you can take any number of paths to visit **Studley Royal**, the formally landscaped 18th-century water park that uses the Skell for its feed. The park was begun by John Aislabie after expulsion from Parliament for his part of the South Sea Bubble scandal in 1720, with the abbey forming part of the vista; his son William completed the scheme – evidently the family had much more skill at landscaping than financial management. The design of the wider estate incorporates the **Deer Park** where you are virtually guaranteed to see some antlered beasts. Once when I visited, the lower branches of the trees around **St Mary's Church**, within the grounds of the estate, were getting a very good pruning. The church itself is a visual treat inside, with an extraordinarily ornate 1870s interior by William Burges (best known for his adornments to Cardiff Castle), and featuring depictions of angelic musicians and carved parrots against a gorgeous background of red and gold.

Visitors to Fountains Abbey and Studley Royal arriving on the Ripon Roweller bus 139 from Ripon Bus Station, running on Sundays and bank holidays from April to October, receive half-price entry. You can also walk into Studley Royal via public footpaths, in particular the delightfully secretive Skell Valley; Studley Roger is a useful starting point. The licensed restaurant at Fountains serves homemade dishes from locally sourced produce.

10 NEWBY HALL

☎ 01423 322583 ⁑ http://newbyhallandgardens.com; closed in winter.

Arriving by car, bike or on foot (the Ripon Rowel Walk runs close to the estate), you enter through the majestic parkland, splattered with giant oak trees, under which cattle and sheep fill their bellies. After an eternally long driveway, you're greeted with the great brick Georgian façade of the hall, an imposing front entrance that looms large. There are guided tours of the house, while you can wander at will around the equally impressive gardens, split into themed 'rooms' with one of the longest herbaceous borders you're likely to encounter.

It's the 'extras' that help to keep a place like Newby Hall financially viable, but all too often the added 'attractions' of miniature railways, adventure playgrounds and craft fairs can detract from the beauty of this place.

Shopping and dining are possible at Newby Hall but, oddly, you have to pay for entrance to the gardens to access the shop or restaurant. There is also **Newby Hall Farm Shop** (☎ 01423 326452 ⁑ http:// newbyhallfarmshop.co.uk) off-site, on the B6265 near Boroughbridge.

¶¶ FOOD & DRINK

Black Lion Skelton on Ure ☎ 01423 322516 ⁑ www.blacklionskelton.co.uk. A very welcoming little village pub serving good food and drink on the doorstep of Newby Hall.

11 RIPON

Now that York has gone it alone, North Yorkshire boasts just the one city and believe it or not this is it. Ripon is smaller than most towns, with a great history and that characterful atmosphere that provincial market towns seem to acquire. It owes its status to its huge cathedral, one that dominates its surroundings and is vastly out of proportion to the city's size, a sign of the cathedral's importance. You can see **Ripon Cathedral** as you approach from the surrounding roads – and the chances are you will approach the city this way, for the railway no longer reaches Ripon.

THE RIPON HORNBLOWER

The Ripon Hornblower is the product of 1,000 years of history, when the wakeman was responsible for security, particularly at night. He could impose fines or would have to provide compensation to victims should, for example, a burglary occur during his overnight watch. The job of wakeman effectively became outdated by the 16th century, but even so, the Ripon Hornblower still calls his tune every night at 21.00 around the four corners of the obelisk in the market square.

Your only other option is by boat – either on the River Ure or on the Ripon Canal, itself a tiny 2½-mile spur that enters town off the Ure.

Ripon Cathedral

http://riponcathedral.info.

The official title for Ripon's most imposing structure is the cathedral church of St Peter and St Wilfrid. The city recently celebrated 1,300 years of Wilfrid's connections with the cathedral; he became abbot of a Benedictine monastery on the site and built a new church (new in AD672, that is). The crypt of that church, the oldest existing Saxon crypt in England, forms the basis of today's cathedral; it became a place of pilgrimage because of the saint. The crypt was built to resemble Christ's tomb as Wilfrid imagined it. It's a tiny, whitewashed room with a ledge for a candle; so very different to the embellishments and adornments that grace the building above. One visitor asked, as he squeezed down the narrow, dimly lit staircase, 'Is this it?' I'm not sure quite what he was expecting to see; indeed, that is all you get, except for a sense of over a thousand years of history.

"It's a tiny, whitewashed room with a ledge for a candle; so very different to the embellishments and adornments that grace the building above."

The cathedral is at the centre of Ripon life, just as it has always been. Its history lies within the tombs – the remains of ancient families of significance, such as the Markenfield family from nearby Markenfield Hall (see page 161). But, like many huge structures of significant age in need of a new identity, it fulfils the differing roles today of art gallery, concert hall and meeting place. Musicians are regularly making the most of the cathedral's acoustics, not least during the free Thursday lunchtime concerts.

Ripon's museums

All three museums: ☎ 01765 690799 🖰 www.riponmuseums.co.uk; special reduced-rate ticket for all museums.

Opposite the cathedral is the **Courthouse Museum** (Minster Road), one of three museums linked by their subject matter; the others, five minutes' walk away, are the **Workhouse Museum** (Allhallowgate) and the **Prison and Police Museum** (St Marygate). The titles are a dead giveaway to the buildings and the content, but they have played an important part in the history of the city. Ripon maintained independence from the rest of Yorkshire until 1888, so it had to provide its own law and order. In the courthouse (operational until 1998), you can stand in the dock and listen to a court session where petty thieves were sentenced with deportation to Australia. In the workhouse, you can try your hand at the same toil that was expected of the Victorian paupers while the prison has some horrific tales of punishment and regime, all the more terrifying when the five-inch thick door is slammed shut.

Walking around Ripon

Wandering around Ripon is a pleasure. It has an eclectic mix of both stone and brick buildings of every conceivable style and yet, owing to the nature of the materials used, even recently built houses seem to blend in well with the existing structures and streets.

If you fancy a quiet stroll, head to the **Ripon Spa Gardens**, a small but verdant oasis. The main entrance (wheelchair accessible) is on Park Street, with other, stepped entrances off Skellbank. A combination of flower borders, grassy picnic spots and mature trees centred around a traditional bandstand provides somewhere to munch a pork pie from

"There's a splendid Art Nouveau decorated entrance hall, complete with stained glass, the likes of which you never see in any modern leisure complex."

Appletons (see page 166). Regardless of any intention to dip a toe, if you're passing the impressive ornate, brick building that houses the old (but still operational) **swimming baths**, next door to the Park Street entrance of the spa gardens, poke your head around the door; there's a splendid Art Nouveau decorated entrance hall, complete with stained glass, the likes of which you never see in any modern leisure complex. It's the **River Laver** that runs through the centre of the city, joining up with the River Ure on the outskirts, and the **Ripon Canal** runs adjacent to the Laver, on the opposite side of the Boroughbridge Road. The **canal basin**, accessed off Bondgate Green and Canal Road on foot, is hidden away and looks rather lonely despite it being only five minutes' walk from the town centre.

The **marketplace and cathedral** is as good a place as any to begin a walk. Indeed a set of waymarked routes begins at the cathedral. The **Sanctuary Way Walk** is based upon the times when Ripon looked after its own law and anyone within the Sanctuary Boundary, marked by a series of posts (one of which still stands today), was granted overnight sanctuary. New markers have been installed, not so much to grant sanctuary to tourists, but to encourage walkers around the town and its outer limits through the countryside. The full circuit is ten miles long but there are shorter walks that visit historically important locations. You can pick up a route map (although the walks are marked) from the **tourist information centre** opposite the entrance to the cathedral.

"The Sanctuary Way Walk is based upon the times when Ripon looked after its own law and anyone within the Sanctuary Boundary was granted overnight sanctuary."

For a much longer walk, the **Ripon Rowel Walk**, which passes the cathedral, uses 50 miles of existing public rights of way or permissive paths on a wander through the extended countryside around Ripon. *En route*, you walk through beautiful villages and some lovely, gentle countryside, past river valleys, lakes and one or two impressive buildings such as Markenfield Hall and Fountains Abbey. The most accessible bit of it is the three-mile stretch that follows the full length of the Ripon Canal towpath towards Newby Hall.

¶ FOOD & DRINK

Appleton's Market Pl ✆ 01765 603198. Pork butchers selling the most fantastic pork pies. The best I've ever tasted – dare I say, far better than any Melton Mowbray pie.

The Old Deanery Minster Rd ✆ 01765 600003 🖰 www.theolddeanery.co.uk. Up-market restaurant in a beautiful Grade 2 listed building adjacent to the cathedral. The cooking makes much use of local produce and the chef has worked under Gary Rhodes.

The One-eyed Rat Allhallowgate ✆ 01765 607704 🖰 www.oneeyedrat.com. A popular town boozer; no food but great beer. Regular quiz and occasional live music and beer festivals.

The Water Rat Bondgate Green ✆ 01765 602251 🖰 www.thewaterrat.co.uk. Near the town centre but hidden away on the banks of the River Skell. A food-orientated pub but the beer is up to scratch as well.

12 WENSLEYDALE IN NIDDERDALE: KIRKBY MALZEARD & AROUND

⌂ The Ruin Grewelthorpe (see page 177)

Within the Nidderdale AONB a cluster of villages and hamlets here are not directly on the well-known tourist trail, which is partly what makes their character so appealing. This is an area to savour on a bike, along quiet country lanes. I love the quietness of **Laverton**, on the River Laver, and the **Grantley** villages. But my favourite is **Kirkby Malzeard**, one of the larger villages in the area with a long main street and lots of footpaths disappearing off into the fields.

"The trail is based upon a community project set up when a group of residents calling themselves 'The Crackpots' created a series of mosaic pictures depicting important aspects of local life."

There's a great circular walk just west of Kirkby Malzeard called the **Crackpots Mosaic Trail**. It's 6½ miles long and is based around **Dallowgill**, an area known for its Iron Age forts. The trail is based upon a community project set up in Kirkby Malzeard when a group of residents calling themselves 'The Crackpots' created a series of mosaic pictures depicting important aspects of local life. These 22 mosaics have been placed around the trail and make excellent waypoints as well as bringing in a treasure hunt – great with children. The mosaics include pictures of wildlife and flora that are likely to be encountered along the way.

The walk extends through woodlands, along tracks, over rivers and streams, along field ditches and up over moorland. It's not suitable for cycling but if your feet will hold out, carry on along the road from the pub, slightly further southwest, up and across **Skelding Moor**. It's a tiny area of moorland that was once used for quarrying and mining – though much of that evidence has gone. From the top of the moor there are some wonderful views across Upper Nidderdale in the west and right the way across to the North York Moors. On a clear day you can just make out the White Horse carving on the edge of the **Hambleton Hills**.

⫿ FOOD & DRINK

The Grantley Arms High Grantley HG4 3PJ ✆ 01765 620227 ⌂ www.grantleyarms.com. Pleasant pub with a panelled bar and a real log fire.

SWINTON PARK COOKERY SCHOOL

Swinton Park, near Masham HG4 4JH ✆ 01765 680900 ⌂ www.swintonpark.com.

A part of the spectacularly imposing Swinton Park hotel just outside Masham, the cookery school here is open to both day visitors and hotel residents alike. Housed in the renovated Georgian stables overlooking the crenellated castle entrance, this is a cookery school with a difference.

The kitchen has quite an informal, homely feel, like a personal farmhouse kitchen complete with a huge AGA as the centrepiece. Students prepare and cook food around a giant central table, topped with a slab of smooth granite just waiting for some pastry and a rolling pin. After the hard work has been done, you adjourn to the cookery school's fine dining room (not your average school dining room), where the food that you prepared is served to you. If you have a partner who has been keeping well out of the way for the duration of the course, they can join you in the dining room to taste your culinary delights.

Day courses cover all kinds of tastes and techniques: there's a bread-making course, or you can learn how to make the ultimate Sunday lunch, and they run children's cookery courses too, including private family tuition for groups of two adults and two children who like to cook together.

See also *Accommodation,* page 177.

13 MASHAM

⌂ **Swinton Park** (see page 177)

⚑ **Bivouac** (see page 177) and **The Old Station Yard** (see page 178)

I can't understand why the small market town of Masham doesn't make it into the Yorkshire Dales National Park. To me it is the epitome of Dales life, a town with true community spirit that holds its traditions dearly while moving forward. Arrive on any given day and you could be witnessing Yorkshire cricket, judging sheep or supping a pint of the local brew – from not one but two breweries.

"I often judge a town by its shops. From them, you can tell the character of the place."

I often judge a town by its shops. From them, you can tell the character of the place. In Masham there is no supermarket (except for a tiny Co-op) and the town is all the better for it. Instead, tucked between the old stone houses that line the market square, is a bakery, a butchers and a greengrocers, one after the other. And there are often people queuing out of the door from each shop. I was ecstatic to see this, not so much that I would have to wait a little while to purchase the most delicious looking, locally grown strawberries, but that the residents obviously value their way of life.

Masham is officially part of Wensleydale, bordering the **River Ure**, though it is many miles from the area that most think of as being Wensleydale, around Hawes. The Ure by now is a sizeable river, a rowing boat or a swim required to get from one bank to the other. On entering Masham from Ripon, you cross over the Ure before it flows past the recreation ground and cricket ground. Sitting listening to the river gurgling behind you, this is an idyllic place to pause for a while or catch up on a few runs, the cricket club regularly serving afternoon teas at weekends during a match.

The breweries

Beer has placed Masham on the map. The older of the two breweries is **Theakston** (✆01765 680000 🖰 www.theakstons.co.uk) renowned for its 'Old Peculier' ale. Established in 1827, the brewery is still under the ownership of the Theakston family, although a brief spell with a multi-national conglomerate before being bought back by the Theakstons split the family. From the visitor centre, named the **Black Bull in Paradise** (you'll find out why when you visit) you can take a guided tour of the old Victorian brewery concluding, naturally, with sampling some of the ales in the visitor centre bar. Though what really interests me is the cooperage, with the brewery having one of the few remaining craft coopers in the country; it's fascinating to see how they make the traditional barrels.

However, there is another side to the story of brewing in Masham. When Theakstons was sold to an international corporation for a while, it caused friction within the Theakston clan and one family member, Paul Theakston, decided to go it alone. He set up a rival brewery in the town using traditional brewing methods. With Masham's long association with sheep (the traditional sheep fair is still held in the town annually), and the background to the brewery's formation, it was named the **Black Sheep Brewery**. It too is now a massive part of Yorkshire life with worldwide fame. As with their rival, you can take a tour of the brewery here and compare notes of the two brewing houses, although there should be no industrial espionage required; the family members have 'kissed and made up'!

"The Black Sheep Brewery is now a massive part of Yorkshire life with worldwide fame."

¶¶ FOOD & DRINK

Black Sheep Brewery Visitor Centre Wellgarth ✆ 01765 680101 ⬦ www.
blacksheepbrewery.co.uk. On the site of the brewery (you can smell the hops as you enter),
there's a bistro serving food all day and evening meals. The bar serves the ales.

Mad Hatters' Tea Room 2 Church St ✆ 01765 689129. Traditional tea room serving
morning coffee, lunches and afternoon tea.

The White Bear Hotel Wellgarth ✆ 01765 689319 ⬦ www.thewhitebearhotel.co.uk.
The Theakston's Brewery tap, serving their full range of beers, in a building bizarrely attached
to the Black Sheep Brewery. Excellent food and dog-friendly B&B accommodation.

14 DRUID'S TEMPLE

West of Masham, a narrow lane rising from the village of Ilton heads up
in to forest plantation and abruptly stops. Follow the remaining track
and very soon you may find yourself blinking in disbelief at a bizarre
curio that is the folly of all follies: a scaled-down Stonehenge plonked
amid the trees. Actually it's Stonehenge with knobs on – more lintels
than the real thing, and a stone table, cave and altar to boot. Only it's far
from prehistoric, having been created by the local landowner, William
Danton, in the 1820s as a job creation scheme. He even engaged
someone to play the role of a hermit, though it's said that whoever took
on the role didn't stick it out for long before going slightly off the rails.

ACCOMMODATION

The accommodation recommended in this book is of course by no means exhaustive, as there is a huge range of places to stay in the Yorkshire Dales. Those featured are my personal choice, with no charge having been made by the businesses concerned. I have tried to select a range to suit different pockets, from basic camping to outrageous luxury; and styles – some bed and breakfast, some self-catering, and some for larger groups. All however, I feel are 'special' in some way, historically, architecturally or perhaps with a particular 'Slow' take on things.

The hotels, B&Bs and self-catering options featured in this section are indicated by 🏠 under the heading for the town or village in which they are located. Campsites are indicated by 🔺. Where a recommended pub or tea room offers accommodation I have mentioned it in the listing.

1 THREE PEAKS

Hotel

The Traddock Austwick LA2 8BY ☎ 01524 251224 🖰 www.thetraddock.co.uk. This neat Georgian stone building doubles as a luxury country house hotel with an enviable reputation for very English, period comfort. It was built by the locally influential Ingleby family on a field known as the trading paddock, hence the weird abbreviated nickname. All the rooms are en-suite doubles bar one single, and room rates are reasonable. Dogs are welcome for a small fee.

B&Bs

Cross Keys Inn Cautley LA10 5NE ☎ 01539 620284 🖰 www.cautleyspout.co.uk. This 400-year-old temperance inn was left to the National Trust in the will of Mrs Edith Adelaide Bunney in the year 1949. She was the last in a long line of Quaker owners but the present tenant, Alan Clowes, carries on the tradition describing himself as 'a vociferous Quaker'. The inn has two available rooms (one twin, one family) which are both old-fashioned and homely. Rates are very reasonable and, as you might expect from such a well regarded eating house, the breakfasts are fabulous. No dogs.

Garsdale B&B Garsdale LA10 5PU ☎ 01969 667096 🖰 www.thegarsdale.com. Converted barn with three rooms (double, twin and family) attached to the owners' house and restaurant where magnificent breakfasts are served. Evening meals and residents bar available but there is a good pub (Moorcock Inn) next door anyway. If you are travelling without a car, the owners will pick you up free of charge from Garsdale station (on the Settle–Carlisle line). They also run a charged drop-off and pick-up service for walkers and, as the Pennine Bridleway goes past the door, very thoughtfully provide bike repair and storage facilities and even a field for tethering your horses. Dog-friendly (one room only).

Old Hill Inn Chapel le Dale LA6 3AR   01524 241256   www.oldhillinn.co.uk. Legendary old inn (see page 36) once frequented by Winston Churchill. Standard, good value B&B upstairs and a small camping/caravan site behind the pub. Dog-friendly throughout.

Self-catering

Bower Bank EcoBarn Gawthrop, Dent LA10 5QQ   01539 625707   www.bowerbank-ecobarn.com. This is a self-catering venue with gilt-edged 'Eco' credentials: all hot water and under-floor heating comes from a ground source heat pump, a wood-burning stove keeps you toasty on extra cold nights and rain water flushes the toilets. The address may be Gawthrop, Dent but in reality Bower Bank sits in splendid isolation halfway up the hillside, with extensive views down the dale and up to Combe Scar behind. A former recording studio of musician/comedian/rambler and general good egg Mike Harding, this beautiful old stone building is now in the keeping of Justin and Virginia Walker who live in the farm next door. Sleeps up to ten with an extra two in the farm annex if required. Dog-friendly (big garden)

Deeside House Dentdale LA10 5RN   01539 625251   www.deesidehouse.co.uk. I remember this as a youth hostel back in the 1980s, but before then it was a shooting lodge. Now it's a week or weekend self-catering venue ideal for large groups like extended families or walking groups as it sleeps up to 32 in seven en-suite rooms. All the old youth hostel facilities are still there (15 bathrooms and a games room) but comfort levels have dramatically improved. The isolated riverside location is idyllic but civilisation (The Sportsmans Inn) is less than a mile's stroll away. Dog-friendly.

Lock Bank Farm Howgill Lane, Sedbergh LA10 5HE   01539 620252   http://daleswayluxuryices.co.uk. If you like your peace and quiet but don't want to be too far from amenities then this place fits the bill. It's only just in Sedbergh, the last building on the Howgill road before the hillside climbs steeply up to the summit of Winder but the shops and pubs of town are a mere half mile stroll away. The Mount is the old farmhouse available to sleep eight self-catering. An added bonus for those with a sweet tooth is that Howgill Fellside Dairy Ice Cream (see page 39) is produced on the farm. A working farm, so no dogs allowed.

Campsite

Holme Farm Sedbergh LA10 5ET   01539 620654   www.holmeopenfarm.co.uk. One of David and Angela Metcalfe's farm fields doubles as a quiet, cheap and cheerful family-friendly campsite. As this is an open farm there are lots of children's activities involving contact with the farm animals. The on-site café also sells basic camping supplies. The owners are quite strict on the 'quiet after dark' rule, which suits me as I hate noisy campsites. Consequently, rowdy adult groups are not welcome and, as this is a working farm, neither are dogs.

2 CRAVEN & WHARFEDALE
B&B

Knowles Lodge B&B Appletreewick BD23 6DQ ☏ 01756 720228 ⌂ www.knowleslodge.com. A timber-framed house in 18 acres of grounds on the banks of the River Wharfe. The Knowles-Fitton family, of running up hills fame (see box, page 73), offer luxury B&B at an affordable price in a choice of twin, double or family room. If you love the setting but prefer your tent, there is basic camping in the field by the river. Your hosts, Chris and Pam also have fly-fishing rights to a stretch of the river which is available to guests. Children aged seven or over are welcome, as are dogs.

Self-catering

Airton Meeting House Aireton BD23 4AE ☏ 01729 830263 ⌂ http://airtonbarn.org.uk. This 17th-century Friends' Meeting House, possibly the oldest in the world still used for worship, has an old stable block converted into a six-bed bunkroom.

Barden Bunkbarn Barden BD23 6AS ☏ 01756 720616 ⌂ www.bardenbunkbarn.co.uk. A sole-use, very comfortable bunk barn sleeping up to 24 people in four rooms. The building is part of the Grade 1 listed Barden Tower complex. Many groups stay here after dining at the Priest's House Restaurant next door (see page 70) but it's also ideal for cycling/walking parties or extended families. No dogs.

Beamsley Hospital Almshouse Beamsley, near Bolton Abbey BD23 6HQ ☏ 01628 825925 ⌂ www.landmarktrust.org.uk. The Landmark Trust specialises in unusual buildings, and this one is certainly that. It is circular and all on one storey with seven rooms, three of which are bedrooms (double, twin and single). What makes it unique is that these rooms all radiate out from a central chapel that has to be crossed on any journey from room to room. Originally built in Elizabethan times by the famous Lady Ann Clifford's mother, it was lived in by nuns right up until the 1970s – they may have gone but the chapel bell remains. Very expensive; dog-friendly.

Cowside Langstrothdale, BD23 5JE ☏ 01628 825925 ⌂ www.landmarktrust.org.uk . This 16th-century farmstead was taken on by the National Trust to preserve its historic value – in particular a monumental inglenook fireplace and rare wall painting in the parlour. The Landmark Trust lease the building and offer it as a self-catering cottage to sleep five people in three bedrooms. This is the place for you if you value isolation, as the nearest hamlet of Hubberholme is four miles away and the house is only accessible by foot (150 yards from the road). Expensive, but special and dog-friendly too.

3 SWALEDALE
B&B

Tan Hill Inn Tan Hill, near Reeth DL11 6ED ✆ 01833 628246 🔍 www.tanhillinn.
co.uk. A wide range of accommodation is on offer at this 'highest pub in Britain' (see page 97), from very cheap camping or a bunk in a barn, to self-catering in the Drover's Rest flat or good value traditional B&B above the pub. It can be either really quiet or wild here (the latter if there's a musical event on – check before booking). Dogs are allowed in some rooms.

Self-catering

Culloden Tower Richmond DL10 4XL ✆ 01628 825925 🔍 www.landmarktrust.org.uk. Holidaying in this incredibly ornate 16th-century building, rented out by the Landmark Trust, was described by one visitor as like 'staying in a giant Wedgewood vase'. Its parkland location overlooking the River Swale is both magnificent and convenient as the facilities of the town are only five minutes' walk away. The building consists of four floors with just one octagonal room on each, all linked by a spiral staircase. Two of the rooms are bedrooms sleeping four people in total (double and twin). Extremely expensive but unique. Dog-friendly.

Dales Bike Centre Fremington DL11 6AW ✆ 01748 884908 🔍 www.dalesbikecentre.
co.uk. The friendly team here offers very affordable B&B (bunk and breakfast) walking distance from Reeth. The accommodation comes as two or four beds per room (single with a supplement). As you might expect, everything is set up brilliantly for cyclists and walkers, with facilities for bike washing, secure storage, drying room and laundry, but anyone is welcome here and in the café next door. No dogs in rooms.

Keld Bunkbarn and Yurts Park House, Keld DL11 6DZ ✆ 01748 886549 🔍 www.
keldbunkbarnandyurts.com. A variety of accommodation is on offer here, from cheap and cheerful bunk rooms for two, three or four to traditional bring-your-own tent camping. What has become their most popular summer option is one of two 19-foot Mongolian-style yurts, described by one visitor as 'adventurous like camping but luxurious like a hotel.' Each is heated by a wood-burning stove and can comfortably accommodate four people on real beds – you even have the option of a continental breakfast and/or evening meal delivered to your door. Dogs welcome.

Old Cello Workshop The Green, Richmond DL10 4RG ✆ 01748 825525 🔍 www.
yorkshirecountryholiday.co.uk. A former cello-makers' premises is now a self-catering cottage sleeping six in three bedrooms (two doubles and a twin) for a reasonable price. It has a perfect location, in a quiet corner of town by the river and with views of Culloden Tower (see above) out back, but less than five minutes' walk from the Market Square. Children and dogs welcome.

Campsite

Rukin's Campsite Keld DL11 6LJ ✆ 01748 886274 🖰 www.rukins-keld.co.uk. Basic camping but on a glorious riverside site, with Catrake Force waterfall on the premises and Kisdon Force just downstream. The River Swale here is a wild-swimmers' delight with deep plunge pools galore but also gentle pebbly sections where the children can paddle. The campsite has a toilet block with free showers and a provisions-store-cum-café. Dog-friendly.

4 WENSLEYDALE

B&Bs

The Blue Lion East Witton DL8 4SN ✆ 01969 624273 🖰 www.thebluelion.co.uk. Each of the 15 rooms here has a slightly different design and feel to the others but they are all en-suite, very comfortable and not outrageously expensive. Some are in the old stables annex (dogs welcome) while the rest are in the main house. Downstairs happens to be a smashing old pub with an excellent restaurant (see page 130).

Green Dragon Inn Hardraw DL8 3LZ ✆ 01969 667392 🖰 www.greendragonhardraw.com. This is a good pub with a long and interesting history but what makes it unique is the waterfall in the back garden (see page 115). Choices of accommodation style suit all tastes and pockets, from camping and bunk room to self-catering and B&B. Wordsworth and Turner both stayed here and the poshest suites are named after those two venerable chaps. Everything on offer is good value.

Self-catering

Gill Edge Cottages Gill Edge, Bainbridge DL8 3DB ✆ 01969 650367 🖰 www.gilledgecottages.com. A mile up the hill from Bainbridge village, the old farm of Gill Edge has three basic but very affordable self-catering cottages on-site, each to sleep four people in two bedrooms. The Wensleydale Equestrian Centre also operates from Gill Head so if you were planning to go horseriding during your visit then why not have it on your doorstep. Extensive grounds are open for guests to enjoy, including a summer house and woods sloping down to the River Bain. Two of the cottages are dog-friendly.

Temple Folly Swinithwaite DL8 4UH ✆ 01969 663249 🖰 www.templefolly.co.uk. This singular little Georgian building has been a hunting lodge and summer house in its past but the name refers to a nearby 11th-century Knights Templar chapel. Part of the Swinithwaite Hall Estate, it has been renovated recently to become a self-catering cottage for two. The building comprises two octagonal rooms only (one above the other) and a balcony. Its location is just off the A684 but hidden in its own copse of trees a stone's throw from the River Ure – trout fly-fishing is available to residents. Staying in Temple Folly is not cheap but then you are paying for a very unusual experience. No dogs allowed.

5 NIDDERDALE, HARROGATE & AROUND

Hotel

Swinton Park Swinton, near Masham HG4 4JH ☎ 01765 680900 ♙ www.swintonpark. com. This is a country house hotel specialising in unashamed opulence. The cheapest room is nearly £200 for B&B (I had to smile at the charge for having your dog in your room – more than I paid for B&B for myself recently). Having said that, everything about the place – the restaurant, grounds, rooms and service – is top-class. Added extras to your experience when staying here could be taking part in one of the many events here like food fairs, garden design days or falconry displays. Alternatively, you could sign up for golf, fishing, shooting or one of the famous cookery school courses (see page 168).

Self-catering

Bewerley Hall Cottage Bewerley HG3 5JA ☎ 01765 688210 ♙ www.cottageinbewerley. com. Rustic, snug and homely are the three words that most spring to mind, especially on cold days when the wood-burning stove is roaring away. Self-catering cottages for just two people are few and far between and all-too-often you end up paying for bedrooms you don't use. This ex-Bewerley Hall gardener's cottage offers quality at a fair price and in a handy position – a short walk into Pateley Bridge town or out into the local woods and fells. One double bedroom. Dogs welcome.

The Ruin Grewelthorpe HG4 3DE ☎ 01628 825925 ♙ www.landmarktrust.org.uk. Don't be put off by the name of the building or village because this is a brilliant place owned by the Landmark Trust, in a great location and available to rent self-catered for two people in one double bedroom. The building was always designed to be two things at once, a lavish Georgian garden pavilion in the Gothic style at the front, and a mock Roman ruin at the back. And it is the back that I feel has The Ruin's best feature – its spectacular view over the wooded gorge of Hackfall below and the hills beyond. Great walking is to be had from the door and Grewelthorpe's fine pub is a stroll-able mile away. Landmark Trust properties are never cheap and this is no exception. No dogs.

Campsites

Bivouac Near Masham HG4 4JY ☎ 01765 535020 ♙ www.thebivouac.co.uk. I hate the term 'glamping' but I love this place. This is not glamorous camping (no electricity in the shacks and yurts) but is, as the operators put it, 'rustic, luxurious, sustainable and thoughtful'. The accommodation choices are woodland shack (sleeps seven in five rooms), meadow yurt (sleeps five in four rooms) or bunk barn (the whole room for 12 or just a bed). Eco-ethos is taken very seriously with wood-burning stoves and boilers the only heating and lots of recycling of things like waste and grey water – even the décor isn't immune from the re-use and restore policy and has been described as 'shabby chic'. There's a definite overall feel of hippiness, in the nicest possible way. Prices are reasonable and the site, near the Druid's Temple, has its own café.

The Old Station Yard Masham HG4 4DF 📞 01765 689659 🖱 www.oldstation-masham. com. What was the old town railway station is now a basic caravan/campsite but also that rarity in the genre – quiet, friendly, clean, efficient and good value. The old goods shed is now reception, tea room, shop and railway museum while the former engine shed is the immaculate toilet and shower block. The Old Station Yard is actually in the hamlet of Low Burton but the bright lights of Masham town are only half a mile's footpath stroll away. Dogs are welcome but must be kept on leads on-site.

PHOTOGRAPHERS

INDEX

Page numbers in **bold** refer to major entries.